Berlitz®

Malay

phrase book & dictionary

Berlitz Publishing

New York   London   Singapore

Contacting the Editors

Every effort has been made to provide accurate information in this publication, but changes are inevitable. The publisher cannot be responsible for any resulting loss, inconvenience or injury. We would appreciate it if readers would call our attention to any errors or outdated information. We also welcome your suggestions; if you come across a relevant expression not in our phrase book, please contact us at: **comments@berlitzpublishing.com**

Printed in China

Editor: Zara Sekhavati
Translation: updated by Wordbank
Cover Design: Rebeka Davies
Interior Design: Beverley Speight
Picture Researcher: Beverley Speight
Cover Photos: all images Shutterstock

Interior Photos: All photos APA James Tye except - istock p13, 16, 47, 49, 50, 60, 61, 71, 90, 91, 123, 124, 142, 153, 154, 157, 159, 160, 163, 165; APA Mina Patria p25; APA Britta Jaschinski p46, 86; APA Bev Speight p55; APA A Nowitz p96; APA Corrie Wingate p108; APA Kate Browne p180.

Distribution

UK, Ireland and Europe
Apa Publications (UK) Ltd
sales@insightguides.com
United States and Canada
Ingram Publisher Services
ips@ingramcontent.com
Australia and New Zealand
Woodslane
info@woodslane.com.au
Southeast Asia
Apa Publications (SN) Pte
singaporeoffice@insightguides.com

Worldwide
Apa Publications (UK) Ltd
sales@insightguides.com

Special Sales, Content Licensing, and CoPublishing

Discounts available for bulk quantities. We can create special editions, personalized jackets, and corporate imprints. sales@insightguides.com; www.insightguides.biz

Contents

Food & Drink

People

Leisure Time

Special Requirements

In an Emergency

Dictionary

Pronunciation

This section is designed to make you familiar with the sounds of the Malay language using our simplified phonetic transcription. You'll find the pronunciation of the letters and sounds in Malay explained below, together with their 'imitated' equivalents. This system is used throughout the phrase book; simply read the pronunciation as if it were English, noting any special rules below.

Malay, also known as Bahasa Malaysia or Bahasa Melayu, is an Austronesian language also spoken in Indonesia, Singapore, Brunei, the Philippines and southern Thailand. It is written in the Latin alphabet and is an easy language to learn. Words are pronounced as they are spelt. Note that spelling however can be tricky as street names for example can often have different spellings. E.g. the standard Malay for *street* is **baru**, but it can appear as **bahru**, **bharu** and **baharu**. You will come across Sanskrit, Arabic, Tamil, Portuguese, Dutch, Chinese and English words in Malay. English words are increasingly being incorporated into the language, especially in relation to business and technology. The indigenous people retain their own languages.

Consonants

Generally, consonants in the Malay language sound like their English counterparts. In fact, all these consonants sound pretty much the same in Malay and English – **b d f g h j k l m n p r s t v w y z**. The only exception is **c**, which sounds like the 'ch' in 'charm'.

Consonant Combinations

Two consonant combinations are common in the Malay language.
The combination **ng** sounds like the 'ng' in 'ring'
It can occur at the start, in the middle, or at the end of a word.

wide open (mouth)	**nganga** *ngah-ngah*
hand	**tangan** *tah-ngahn*
easy	**senang** *ser-nahng*

*Take note that this combination is not equivalent to the sequence of '**n**' followed by '**g**' in the English word '**finger**'. When this sequence of sounds is needed in Malay, it is spelt **ngg** as in **tangguh**.

The combination **ny** sounds like '**ny**' in '**banyan**' or '**ni**' in '**onion**'.
It can occur at the start or in the middle of a word.

| fresh (environment) | **nyaman** *nyah-mahn* |
| smile | **senyum** *ser-nyum* |

Vowels

The pronunciation of Malay vowels may be slightly trickier for English speakers.

Letter	Symbol	Approximate Pronunciation	Example (Translation)	Pronunciation
a	**ah**	like '**a**' in 'mama'	**ayam** (chicken)	*ah-yahm*
e	**er**	1. like '**er**' in 'farmer'	**beri** (give)	*ber-ri*
e	**ey**	2. like '**e**' in 'empty'	**meja** (table)	*mey-jah*
i	**i**	like '**i**' in 'sit'	**pagi** (morning)	*pah-gi*
o	**o**	like '**o**' in 'over'	**orang** (people)	*o-rahng*
u	**oo**	1. like '**oo**' in 'fool'	**pusing** (turn)	*poo-sing*
u	**u**	2. like '**u**' in 'full'	**bagus** (good)	*bah-gus*

Diphthongs

In the Malay language, there are also vowel combinations called diphthongs, where the sound is formed by the combination of two vowels in a single syllable. The sound begins as one vowel and moves toward another.

Letter	Symbol	Approximate Pronunciation	Example (Translation)	Pronunciation
ai	**ai**	like '**i**' in 'bite'	**kedai** (store)	*ker-dai*
au	**ow**	like '**ow**' in 'now'	**jauh** (far)	*jowh*
ia	**ee-ya**	like '**ee-ya**'	**ialah** (is)	*ee-ya-lah*

How to use this Book

Sometimes you see two alternatives separated by a slash. Choose the one that's right for your situation.

ESSENTIAL

I'm on vacation [holiday]/business.
Saya datang untuk bercuti/urusan perniagaan.
sah-yah dah-tahng oon-tuk ber-chu-ti/oo-ru-sahn per-niah-gah-ahn

I'm going to...
Saya akan pergi ke... *sah-yah ah-kahn per-gi ker*

I'm staying at the...
Saya akan menginap di Hotel... Hotel.
sah-yah ah-khan mer-ngi-nahp di Ho-teyl

Words you may see are shown in YOU MAY SEE boxes.

YOU MAY SEE...

BUKA *boo-kah* open
TUTUP *too-tup* closed

Any of the words or phrases listed can be plugged into the sentence below.

Communications

Can I...?
Bolehkah saya...? *bo-ley-kah sah-yah*

access the internet
melayari internet *mer-lah-yah-ri in-ter-net*

check e-mail
memeriksa emel *mer-mer-rik-sah ee-meyl*

print
mencetak *mern-cher-tahk*

Malay phrases appear in purple.

Read the simplified pronunciation as if it were English. For more on pronunciation, see page 7.

Dining with Children

Do you have children's portions?
Adakah anda mempunyai hidangan saiz kanak-kanak? *ah-dah-kah ahn-dah merm-poon-yai hi-dah-ngahn sah-iz kah-nahk-kah-nahk*

A highchair/child's seat, please.
Sila berikan kerusi tinggi budak. *si-lah ber-ri-kahn ker-roo-si ting-gi boo-dahk*

Where can I feed the baby?
Di manakah saya boleh menyusu bayi? *di mah-nah-kah sah-yah bo-ley mern-yoo-soo bah-yi*

For Traveling with Children, see page 147.

Related phrases can be found by going to the page number indicated.

There is only one emergency number in Malaysia, **999**, for police, ambulance, fire and rescue services. Major hotels offer medical services for minor ailments. A list of important numbers, including local emergency services, should be available at your hotel or the tourist information office.

Information boxes contain relevant country, culture and language tips.

Expressions you may hear are shown in You May Hear boxes.

YOU MAY HEAR...

Ada apa-apa lagi? *ah-dah ah-pah-ah-pah lah-gi*   Anything else?

Color-coded side bars identify each section of the book.

Survival

Arrival & Departure

ESSENTIAL

I'm on vacation [holiday]/business.	**Saya datang untuk bercuti/urusan perniagaan.** *sah-yah dah-tahng oon-tuk ber-chu-ti/oo-ru-sahn per-niah-gah-ahn*
I'm going to...	**Saya akan pergi ke...** *sah-yah ah-kahn per-gi ker*
I'm staying at the... the...Hotel.	**Saya akan menginap di Hotel...** *sah-yah ah-khan mer-ngi-nahp di Ho-teyl...*

YOU MAY HEAR...

Sila tunjukkan pasport anda.
si-lah toon-juk-kahn pahs-port ahn-dah

Your passport, please.

Apakah tujuan lawatan anda?
ah-pah-kah too-juahn lah-wah-tahn ahn-dah

What's the purpose of your visit?

Di manakah anda menginap?
di mah-nah-kah ahn-dah mer-ngi-nahp

Where are you staying?

Berapa lamakah anda akan berada di sini?
ber-rah-pah lah-mah-kah ahn-dah ah-kan ber-rah-dah di si-ni

How long are you staying?

Kamu datang ke sini dengan siapa?
kah-moo dah-tahng ker si-ni der-gahn siah-pah

Who are you here with?

Border Control

I'm just passing through.	**Saya hanya melalui tempat ini.** *sah-yah hah-nyah mer-lah-lui term-paht ee-ni*

I'd like to declare…	**Saya ingin mengisytiharkan…**
	sah-yah ee-ngin mer-ngi-si-ti-har-kahn
I have nothing to declare.	**Saya tidak ada apa-apa untuk diisytiharkan.**
	sah-yah ti-dahk ah-dah ah-pah-ah-pah oon-tuk di-isi-ti-har-kahn

YOU MAY HEAR…

Ada apa-apa untuk diisytiharkan?	Anything to declare?
ah-dah ah-pah-ah-pah oon-tuk di-isy-ti-har-kahn	
Anda mesti membayar cukai untuk barang ini.	You must pay duty on this.
ahn-dah mers-ti merm-bah-yar choo-kai oon-tuk bah-rahng ee-ni	
Buka beg ini.	Open this bag.
boo-kah beyg ee-ni	

YOU MAY SEE...

KETIBAAN	arrivals
PERLEPASAN	departures
KASTAM	customs
BARANG-BARANG BEBAS CUKAI	duty-free goods
BARANG-BARANG UNTUK DIISYTIHARKAN	goods to declare
TIDAK ADA APA-APA UNTUK DIISYTIHARKAN	nothing to declare
PUSAT IMIGRESEN	immigration centre
POLIS	police

Money

ESSENTIAL

Where's the...? **Di manakah...?**
di mah-nah-kah...

ATM **ATM** *ATM*

bank **bank** *bank*

foreign currency **kaunter pertukaran wang asing**
exchange counter *kown-ter per-too-kah-rahn wahng ah-sing*

When does the bank **Bilakah bank akan dibuka/ditutup?**
open/close? *bi-lah-kah bank ah-kahn di-boo-kah/di-too-tup*

I'd like to change **Saya ingin menukar dollar/pound/euro ke**
dollars/pounds/euros **Ringgit.** *sah-yah ee-ngin mer-noo-kar dol-lar/pound*
into Ringgit. *euro ker Ring-git*

I'd like to cash traveler's **Saya ingin menunaikan cek kembara.**
checks [cheques]. *sah-yah ee-ngin mer-noo-nai-kahn cheyk kerm-bah-rah*

YOU MAY SEE...

The official name for Malaysia's monetary unit is **Ringgit Malaysia** (abbreviated **RM**). This is further divided up into sen. **RM1 = 100 sen**.
Notes: RM1, RM2, RM5, RM10, RM50 and RM100.
Coins: 5, 10, 20, and 50 sen.

At the Bank

I'd like to change money/get a cash advance.	**Saya ingin menukar wang/ mendapatkan wang pendahuluan.** *sah-yah ee-ngin mer-noo-kar wahng/ mern-dah-paht-kahn wahng pern-dah-hoo-luahn*
What's the exchange rate/fee?	**Apakah kadar pertukaran (wang asing)?** *ah-pah-kah kah-dar per-too-kah-rahn (wahng ah-sing)*
I think there's a mistake.	**Saya rasa ada kesilapan.** *sah-yah rah-sah ah-dah ker-si-lah-pahn*
I lost my traveler's cheques.	**Saya kehilangan cek kembara.** *sah-yah ker-hi-lah-ngahn cheyk kerm-bah-rah*
My card...	**Kad kredit saya...** *kahd krey-dit sah-yah*
was lost	**telah hilang** *ter-lah hee-lahng*

was stolen	**telah dicuri** *ter-lah di-choo-ri*
doesn't work	**tidak boleh digunakan**
	ti-dahk bo-ley di-goo-nah-kahn
The ATM ate my card.	**ATM itu menelan kad saya.**
	ATM ee-too mer-ner-lahn kahd sah-yah

For Numbers, see page 173.

It's a good idea to carry a combination of cash, traveler's checks [cheques] and/or a credit card. Cash is essential in more rural areas. Foreign currency can be readily exchanged for Ringgit; the most popular are US dollars, British sterling pounds, euro and Singapore dollars.

YOU MAY SEE...

MASUKKAN KAD DI SINI	insert card here
BATAL	cancel
PADAM	clear
MASUK	insert
PIN	PIN
PENGELUARAN	withdrawal
DARI AKAUN SEMASA	from checking [current] account
DARI AKAUN SIMPANAN	from savings account
RESIT	receipt

Getting Around

ESSENTIAL

How do I get to town?	**Bagaimanakah saya boleh pergi ke bandar?** *bah-gai-mah-nah-kah sah-yah bo-ley per-gi ker bahn-dah*
Where's the...?	**Di manakah...?** *di mah-nah-kah...*
airport	**lapanpan terbang** *lah-pah-ngahn ter-bahng*
train station	**stesen keretapi** *stey-seyn ker-rey-tah-pi*
bus station	**stesen bas** *stey-seyn bahs*
Monorail/ Komuter/ LRT station	**Monorel/KTM Komuter/LRT** *Mo-no-reyl/ KTM Ko-moo-ter/LRT*
How far is it?	**Berapa jauh?** *ber-rah-pah jowh*
Where do I buy a ticket?	**Di manakah saya membeli tiket?** *di mah-nah-kah sah-yah merm-ber-li ti-keyt*
A one-way/return-trip ticket to...	**Tiket sehala/ulang-alik ke...** *ti-keyt ser-hah-lah/ oo-lahng-ah-lik ker*
How much?	**Berapakah harganya?** *ber-rah-pah-kah har-gah-nyah*
Which...?	**...yang mana?** *yahng mah-nah*
gate	**pintu** *pin-too*
line	**barisan** *bah-ri-sahn*
platform	**pelantar** *per-lahn-tar*
Where can I get a taxi?	**Di manakah saya boleh mendapatkan teksi?** *di mah-nah-kah sah-yah bo-ley mern-dah-paht-kahn teyk-si*
Take me to this address.	**Bawa saya ke alamat ini.** *bah-wah sah-yah ker ah-lah-maht ee-ni*
Can I have a map?	**Boleh berikan saya peta?** *bo-ley ber-ri-kahn sah-yah per-tah*

Tickets

When's the ...to...?	**Bilakah...ke...** *bi-lah-kah...ker...*
(first) bus	**bas (pertama)** *bahs (per-tah-mah)*
(next) flight	**penerbangan (berikut)** *per-ner-bah-ngahn (ber-ri-koot)*
(last) train	**keretapi (terakhir)** *ker-rey-tah-pi (ter-ahk-hir)*
Where do I buy a ticket?	**Di manakah saya membeli tiket?** *di mah-nah-kah sah-yah merm-ber-li ti-keyt*
One/Two ticket(s) please.	**Sila berikan satu/dua tiket.** *si-lah ber-ri-kahn sah-too/doo-ah ti-keyt*
For today/tomorrow.	**Untuk hari ini/esok.** *oon-tuk hah-ri ee-ni/ey-sok*
A...ticket.	**Satu tiket...** *sah-too ti-keyt...*
one-way	**sehala** *ser-hah-lah*
return trip	**ulang-alik** *oo-lahng-ah-lik*
first class	**kelas pertama** *ker-lahs per-tah-mah*
business class	**kelas bisnes** *ker-lahs bis-neys*
economy class	**kelas ekonomi** *ker-lahs ee-ko-no-mi*
How much?	**Berapakah harganya?** *ber-rah-pah-kah har-gah-nyah*
Is there a discount for...?	**Ada diskaun untuk...?** *ah-dah dis-kown oon-tuk...*
children	**kanak-kanak** *kah-nahk-kah-nahk*
students	**pelajar** *per-lah-jar*
senior citizens	**warga tua** *wahr-gah too-ah*
tourists	**pelancong** *per-lahn-chong*
The express bus/ express train, please.	**Bas ekspres/kereta api, ya.** *Bahs eks-pres/ ker-rey-tah ar-pee eks-pres, yer.*
The local bus/train, please.	**Bas/kereta api biasa, ya** *Bahs/ker-rey-tah ar-pee bi-ah-sah, yer.*
I have an e-ticket.	**Saya ada tiket elektronik.** *sah-yah ah-dah ti-keyt ee-leyk-tro-nik*

Can I buy...	**Boleh saya beli...** *Bo-ley sah-yah ber-li*
a ticket on the bus/train?	**satu tiket bas/kereta api?** *Sah-too ti-keyt bahs/ker-rey-tah ar-pee*
the ticket before boarding?	**tiket sebelum naik?** *ti-keyt ser-ber-loom na-ik*
How long is this ticket valid?	**Berapa lamakah tempoh sah laku tiket ini?** *ber-rah-pah lah-mah-kah teym-poh sah lah-koo ti-keyt ee-ni*
Can I return on the same ticket?	**Bolehkah saya balik dengan tiket yang sama?** *bo-ley-kah sah-yah bah-lik der-ngahn ti-keyt yahng sah-mah*
I'd like to...my reservation.	**Saya ingin...tempahan saya** *sah-yah ee-ngin...term-pah-han sah-yah*
cancel	**membatalkan** *merm-bah-tahl-kahn*
change	**menukarkan** *mer-noo-kah-kahn*
confirm	**mengesahkan** *meng-nge-sah-kan*

For Time, see page 175.

Plane

How much is a taxi to the airport?	**Berapakah tambang taxi untuk ke lapangan terbang?** *ber-rah-pah-kah tahm-bahng ta-xi oon-tuk ker lah-pah-ngahn ter-bahng*
To...Airport, please.	**Sila ke Lapangan Terbang...** *si-lah ker lah-pah-ngahn ter-bahng...*
My airline is...	**Syarikat penerbangan saya ialah...** *siah-ri-kaht per-ner-bahng-ahn sah-yah ee-ya-lah...*
My flight leaves at...	**Penerbangan saya akan berlepas pada pukul...** *per-ner-bahng-ahn sah-yah ah-kahn ber-ler-pahs pah-dah poo-kool...*

I'm in a rush.	**Saya kesuntukkan masa.** *sah-yah ker-soon-took-kahn mah-sah*
Can you take an alternate route?	**Bolehkah anda menggunakan jalan yang lain?** *bo-ley-kah ahn-dah merng-goo-nah-kahn jah-lahn* *yahng lah-een*
Can you drive faster/ slower?	**Bolehkah anda pandu dengan lebihlaju/perlahan?** *bo-ley-kah ahn-dah pahn-doo der-ngahn ler-bih* *lah-joo/per-lah-han*

YOU MAY HEAR...

Apakah syarikat penerbangan yang anda naiki? *ah-pah-kah siah-ri-kaht per-ner-bahng-ahn* *yahng ahn-dah nai-ki*	What airline are you flying?
Domestik atau antarabangsa? *do-meys-tik ah-tow ahn-tah-rah-bahng-sah*	Domestic or international?
Terminal apa? *ter-mi-nal ah-pah*	What terminal?

Malaysia is well-connected by about 41 airlines to all continents. There are international airports located at **Kuala Lumpur**, **Penang**, **Langkawi**, **Johor Bahru**, **Kuching**, **Kota Kinabalu** and **Labuan**. The main gateway is the **Kuala Lumpur International Airport** (**KLIA**) in Sepang in the state of Selangor. The rest of the country, including **Sabah**, **Sarawak** and the **Federal Territory of Labuan** in East Malaysia, is served by 14 domestic airports and airstrips.

Most domestic airports are serviced by **Malaysian Airlines**, **AirAsia** (budget airline) and **Firefly** (budget airline). Tickets can be booked in advance through the individual company websites or through your local travel agent. (Airport tax and surcharges apply).**MAS Wings** currently provides flights to rural airports in **Sabah** and **Sarawak**. **MAS Wings** is a newly formed subsidiary of **Malaysian Airlines** and operates a fleet of Fokker 50 planes.

YOU MAY SEE...

KETIBAAN	arrivals
PERLEPASAN	departures
TUNTUTAN BAGASI	baggage claim
KESELAMATAN	security
PENERBANGAN DOMESTIK	domestic flights
PENERBANGAN ANTARABANGSA	international flights
MENDAFTAR MASUK	check-in
TIKET ELEKTRONIK	e-ticket check-in
PINTU PERLEPASAN	departure gates
LAPANGAN TERBANG	airport

Checking In

Where's check-in?	**Di manakah untuk mendaftar masuk?**	
	di mah-nah-kah oon-tuk mern-dahf-tahr mah-suk	
My name is...	**Nama saya ialah...** *nah-mah sah-yah ee-ya-lah*	
I'm going to...	**Saya akan pergi ke...** *sah-yah ah-kahn per-gi ker*	
I have...	**Saya ada...** *sah-yah ah-dah...*	
one suitcase	**satu beg pakaian** *sah-too beyg pah-kai-ahn*	
two suitcases	**dua beg pakaian** *doo-ah beyg pah-kai-ahn*	
one piece of hand luggage	**satu bagasi tangan** *sah-too bah-gah-si tah-ngahn*	
How much luggage is allowed?	**Berapakah bagasi yang dibenarkan?**	
	ber-rah-pah-kah bah-gah-si yahng di-ber-nar-kahn	
Is that pounds or kilos?	**Adakah itu paun atau kilo?** *ah-dah-kah ee-tu*	
	pown ah-tow ki-lo	

YOU MAY HEAR...

Yang berikutnya! *yahng ber-ri-koot-nyah*	Next!
Sila tunjukkan passport/tiket anda.	Your passport/ticket,
si-lah toon-juk-kahn pass-port/ ti-keyt ahn-dah	please.
Adakah anda akan mendaftar masuk	Are you checking any
bagasi? *ah-dah-kah ahn-dah ah-kahn*	luggage?
mern-dahf-tahr mah-suk bah-gah-si	
Beg itu terlalu besar untuk dibawa	That's too large for a
masuk ke dalam kapal terbang. *beyg ee-tu*	carry-on [piece of hand
ter-lah-loo ber-sah oon-tuk di-bah-wah	luggage].
mah-suk ker dah-lahm kah-pahl ter-bahng	
Adakah anda sendiri yang mengemaskan	Did you pack these
beg ini? *ah-dah-kah ahn-dah sern-di-ri yahng*	bags yourself?
mer-nger-mahs-kahn beyg ee-ni	

YOU MAY HEAR...

Adakah sesiapa yang memberikan anda apa-apa untuk dibawa? *ah-dah-kah ser-siah-pah yahng merm-ber-ri-kahn ahn-dah ah-pah-ah-pah oon-tuk di-bah-wah*

Did anyone give you anything to carry?

Kosongkan poket anda. *ko-song-kahn po-keyt ahn-dah*

Empty your pockets.

Tanggalkan kasut anda. *tahng-gahl-kahn kah-sut ahn-dah*

Take off your shoes.

Naik kapal terbang sekarang ... *naik kah-pahl ter-bahng ser-kah-rahng...*

Now boarding...

Which terminal?	**Terminal/Pintu yang mana?** *ter-mi-nal/pin-too yahng mah-nah*
Which gate?	**Pintu mana?** *Pin-too mah-nah*
I'd like a window/ an aisle seat.	**Saya inginkan tempat duduk di tepi tingkap/ ruang sayap.** *sah-yah ee-ngin-kahn term-paht doo-duk di ter-pi ting-kahp/roo-ahng sah-yahp*
When do we leave/ arrive?	**Bilakah kita akan berlepas/tiba?** *bi-lah-kah ki-tah ah-kahn ber-ler-pahs/ti-bah*
Is the flight delayed?	**Adakah penerbangan ini ditangguhkan?** *ah-dah-kah per-ner-bahng-ahn ee-ni di-tahng-gooh-kahn*
How late?	**Berapa lewat?** *ber-rah-pah ler-waht*

Luggage

Where is/are...?	**Di manakah...?** *di mah-nah-kah*
the luggage trolleys	**troli bagasi** *tro-li bah-gah-si*
the luggage lockers	**lokar bagasi** *lo-kahr bah-gah-si*

the baggage claim	**tuntutan bagasi** *toon-too-tan bah-gah-si*
My luggage has been lost/stolen.	**Bagasi saya telah hilang/dicuri** *bah-gah-si sah-yah ter-lah hee-lahng/di-choo-ri*
My suitcase is damaged.	**Beg pakaian saya sudah rosak.** *beyg pah-kai-ahn sah-yah soo-dah ro-sahk*

Finding your Way

Where is/are…?	**Di manakah…?** *di mah-nah-kah…*
the currency exchange	**tempat menukar wang asing** *term-paht mer-noo-kah wahng ah-sing*
the car hire	**tempat menyewa kereta** *term-paht mer-nyey-wah ker-rey-tah*
the exit	**pintu keluar** *pin-too ker-loo-ah*
the taxis	**teksi** *teyk-si*
Is there… into town?	**Adakah…ke bandar?** *ah-dah-kah… ker bahn-dar*
a bus	**bas** *bahs*
a train	**keretapi** *ker-rey-tah-pi*
a Monorail/ KTM Komuter/LRT	**Monorel/KTM Komuter/LRT** *mo-no-reyl/k-t-m ko-moo-ter/l-r-t*

For Asking Directions, see page 37.

YOU MAY SEE...

PELANTAR	platforms
KETERANGAN/MAKLUMAT	information
TEMPAHAN	reservations
BILIK MENUNGGU	waiting room
KETIBAAN	arrivals
PERLEPASAN	departures

Train

Where's the train station?	**Di manakah stesen keretapi?** *di mah-nah-kah stey-seyn ker-rey-tah-pi*
How far is it?	**Berapa jauh?** *ber-rah-pah jah-ooh*
Where is/are...?	**Di manakah...?** *di mah-nah-kah...*
the ticket office	**kaunter tiket** *kown-ter ti-keyt*
the information desk	**kaunter keterangan** *kown-ter ker-ter-rahng-ahn*
the luggage lockers	**lokar bagasi** *lo-kahr bah-gah-si*
the platforms	**pelantar** *per-lahn-tar*
Can I have a schedule [timetable]?	**Bolehkah bagi saya jadual waktu perjalanan?** *bo-ley-kah bah-gi sah-yah jah-doo-ahl wahk-too per-jah-lahn-nahn*
How long is the trip?	**Berapa lamakah perjalanan ini?** *ber-rah-pah lah-mah-kah per-jah-lahn-ahn ee-ni*
Is it a direct train?	**Adakah ini keretapi terus?** *ah-dah-kah ee-ni ker-rey-tah-pi ter-roos*
Do I have to change trains?	**Perlukah saya menukar keretapi?** *per-loo-kah sah-yah mer-noo-kar ker-rey-tah-pi*
Is the train on time?	**Adakah keretapi ini tepat pada masanya?** *ah-dah-kah ker-rey-tah-pi ee-ni ter-paht pah-dah mah-sah-nyah*

Departures

Which track [platform] to…?	**Yang manakah pelantar ke…?** *yahng mah-nah-kah per-lahn-tar keh…*
Is this the track [platform]/train to…?	**Adakah ini landasan pelantar/keretapi ke…?** *ah-dah-kah ee-ni per-lahn-tar/ ker-rey-tah-pi ker…*
Where is the track [platform]…?	**Di manakah pelantar…?** *di mah-nah-kah per-lahn-tar…*
Where do I change for…?	**Di manakah saya bertukar ke…?** *di mah-nah-kah sah-yah ber-too-kar ker…*

YOU MAY HEAR…

Naik! *naik*	All aboard!
Sila tunjukkan tiket. *si-lah toon-juk-kahn ti-keyt*	Tickets, please.
Anda perlu bertukar di… *ahn-dah per-loo ber-too-kar di…*	You have to change at…
Perhentian berikutnya, … *per-hern-ti-ahn ber-ri-koot-nyah, …*	Next stop, …

On Board

Can I sit here/open the window?	**Bolehkah saya duduk di sini?** *bo-ley-kah sah-yah doo-duk di si-ni*
That's my seat.	**Itu tempat duduk saya.** *ee-too term-paht doo-duk sah-yah*
Here's my reservation.	**Inilah tempahan saya.** *ee-ni-lah term-pah sah-yah*

Bus

Where's the bus station?	**Di manakah stesen bas?** *di mah-nah-kah stey-seyn bahs*
How far is it?	**Berapa jauh?** *ber-rah-pah jah-ooh*
How do I get to…?	**Bagaimanakah saya boleh pergi ke…** *bah-gai-mah-nah-kah sah-yah bo-ley per-gi ker …*
Is this the bus to…?	**Adakah bas ini pergi ke…?** *ah-dah-kah bahs ee-ni per-gi ker …*
Can you tell me when to get off?	**Bolehkah anda beritahu saya bila untuk turun?** *bo-ley-kah ahn-dah ber-ri-tah-hoo sah-yah bi-lah oon-tuk too-roon*
Do I have to change buses?	**Perlukah saya menukar bas?** *per-loo-kah sah-yah mer-noo-kar bahs*
How many stops to…?	**Berapakah perhentian bas ke…?** *ber-rah-pah-kah per-hern-ti-ahn bahs ker …*
Stop here, please!	**Sila berhenti di sini!** *si-lah ber-hern-ti di si-ni*

YOU MAY SEE…

PERHENTIAN BAS	bus stop
MINTA BERHENTI	request stop
MASUK/KELUAR	enter/exit
CAP TIKET ANDA	stamp your ticket

Generally, there are three types of bus services in Malaysia –
public buses for city transportation, tourist buses for sightseeing,
and inter-state buses for traveling between cities.

Three types of inter-state buses operate in Malaysia: the non-air-
conditioned buses plying between states, the air-conditioned express
buses connecting major towns, and the non-air-conditioned public
buses that provide services within each state.

The public buses in major cities like Kuala Lumpur, Penang and Johor
Bahru are more efficient, as compared to those in smaller towns,
which are less frequent.

Monorail/KTM Komuter/LRT

Where's the Monorail/ KTM Komuter/ LRT station?	**Di manakah stesen Monorel/KTM Komuter/LRT?** *di mah-nah-kah stey-seyn mo-no-reyl/k-t-m ko-moo-ter/l-r-t*
A map, please.	**Sila berikan saya peta.** *si-lah ber-ri-kahn sah-yah per-tah*
Which line for…?	**Jalan keretapi yang manakah ke…?** *jah-lahn ker-rey-tah-pi yahng mah-nah-kah ker . . .*
Which direction?	**Arah yang manakah ke…?** *Ah-rah yahng mah-nah-kah ker . . .*
Do I have to transfer [change]?	**Perlukah saya menukar keretapi?** *per-loo-kah sah-yah mer-noo-kar ker-rey-tah-pi*
Is this the Monorel/KTM Komuter/LRT to…?	**Adakah ini Monorel/KTM Komuter/LRT ke…?** *ah-dah-kah ee-ni mo-no-reyl/k-t-m ko-moo-ter/l-r-t ker*
How many stops to…?	**Berapakah perhentian ke…?** *ber-rah-pah-kah per-hern-ti-ahn ker . . .*
Where are we?	**Di manakah kita?** *di mah-nah-kah ki-tah*

For Tickets, see page 19.

Traveling in and around the city centre of Malaysia's capital, Kuala Lumpur (KL), has been made easier with the availability of three major intra-city commuter train services. The **LRT System** links KL with the adjoining Klang Valley district. The **KTM Komuter** connects the suburban or adjoining districts. **KL Monorail** operates within KL city. There are also two high-speed rail services to the Kuala Lumpur International Airport (KLIA), namely the **KLIA Express** and the **KLIA transit**. All the five train services converge at KL Sentral, the transportation hub in the heart of KL.

Boat & Ferry

When is the ferry to…?	**Bilakah feri ke…?** *bi-lah-kah fey-ri ker …*
Can I take my car?	**Boleh saya ambil kereta saya?** *Bo-ley sah-yah ahm-bil ker-rey-tah sah-yah*
What time is the next sailing?	**Pukul berapa masa bertolak seterusnya?** *Poo-kul ber-ah-pa mah-sah ber-toh-lak ser-ter-rus-nya?*
Can I book a seat/cabin?	**Boleh saya tempah tempat duduk/kabin?** *Bo-ley sah-yah tem-pah tem-pat do-duk/kar-bin?*
How long is the crossing?	**Berapa lama masa menyeberang?** *Ber-ah-pa lah-mah mah-sah mer-nyer-ber-ahng?*

For Tickets, see page 19.

Most major islands off Malaysia's coast can be visited by boat and ferry from the mainland. Boats going out to islands on the east coast generally do not follow schedules, and in the monsoon season (November-February) services may stop altogether. Note that the sea can be choppy just before and after the monsoon season.

YOU MAY SEE...

BOT KESELAMATAN	life boat
JAKET KESELAMATAN	life jacket

Taxi

Where can I get a taxi?	**Di manakah saya boleh mendapatkan teksi?**
	di mah-nah-kah sah-yah bo-ley mern-dah-paht-kahn
	teyk-si
Can you send a taxi?	**Adakah anda ada nombor (telefon) untuk**
	(menempah) teksi? *ah-dah-kah ahn-dah ah-dah*
	nom-bor (tey-ley-fon) oon-tuk (mer-nerm-pah) teyk-si
Do you have the	**Adakah anda ada nombor untuk teksi?**
number for a taxi?	*ah-dah-kah ahn-dah ah-dah nom-bor oon-tuk teyk-si*
I'd like a taxi now/for	**Saya ingin sebuah teksi sekarang/untuk esok**
tomorrow at...	**pada pukul...** *sah-yah ee-ngin ser-boo-ah teyk-si ...*
	ser-kah-rahng/ oon-tuk ey-sok pah-dah poo-kool
Pick me up at...	**Ambil saya di...** *ahm-bil sah-yah di ...*
I'm going to...	**Saya hendak pergi ke...** *sah-yah hern-dahk per-gi ker*
this address	**alamat ini** *ah-lah-maht ee-ni*

YOU MAY HEAR...

Ke mana? *ker mah-nah* — Where to?

Apakah alamatnya? *ah-pah-kah ah-lah-maht-nyah* — What's the address?

Ada bayaran tokok untukwaktu malam/ke lapangan terbang. *ah-dah bah-yah-rahn to-kok oon-tuk wak-too mah-lahm/ker lah-pah-ngahn ter-bahng* — There's a night time/airport surcharge.

the airport	**lapangan terbang** *lah-pah-ngahn ter-bahng*	
the train station	**stesen keretapi** *stey-seyn ker-rey-tah-pi*	
I'm late.	**Saya telah lewat** *sah-yah ter-lah ley-waht*	
Can you drive faster/slower?	**Bolehkah anda pandu denganlebih laju/lebih perlahan?** *bo-ley-kah ahn-dah pahn-doo der-ngahn ler-bih lah-joo/ler-bih per-lah-han*	
Stop/Wait here.	**Berhenti/Tunggu di sini.** *ber-hern-ti/toong-goo di si-ni*	

Taxis, mostly air-conditioned, are readily available and fares are metered, though in some places like the smaller towns or the rural areas, cabbies do not use the meter. In such areas, negotiate the fare before boarding. In cities, taxis can be found at taxi stands or can be flagged down anywhere. If required, taxis can be contracted to travel long-distance across towns or states in Malaysia. There are several companies offering taxi and limousine services in Malaysia. Tipping is not a norm in Malaysia, but will be happily accepted.

How much?	**Berapakah harganya?** *ber-rah-pah-kah har-gah-nyah*
You said it would cost…	**Tadi, anda kata tambangnya ialah…** *tah-di, ahn-dah kah-tah tahm-bahng-nyah ee-ya-lah …*
Keep the change.	**Simpanlah duit baki.** *sim-pahn-lah doo-it bah-ki*

Bicycle, Motorbike & Trishaw

I'd like to hire…	**Saya ingin menyewa…** *sah-yah ee-ngin mer-nyey-wah*
a bicycle	**sebuah basikal** *ser-boo-ah bah-si-kahl*
a moped	**sebuah moped** *ser-boo-ah moped*
a motorcycle	**sebuah motosikal** *ser-boo-ah mo-to-si-kahl*
a trishaw	**sebuah beca** *ser-boo-ah bey-cha*
How much per day/ week?	**Berapakah harga untuk sehari/seminggu?** *ber-rah-pah-kah har-gah oon-tuk ser-hah-ri/ ser-ming-goo*
Can I have a helmet/ lock?	**Bolehkah bagi saya sebuah topi keledar/ mangga?** *bo-ley-kah bah-gi sah-yah ser-boo-ah to-pi ker-ley-dar/mahng-gah*
I have a puncture/ flat tyre.	**Tayar saya bocor.** *Tar-yar sah-yah bow-chor*

Bicycle and motorcycle rentals are not popular in Malaysia. They are usually only available at parks or recreational areas. **Trishaws** are gradually being phased out as the cities become modernized. You will need to agree to a price with the trishaw driver before you get on. Rides within the city or town vary according to the distance.

Car Hire

Where's the car hire?	**Di manakah tempat untuk menyewa kereta?** *di mah-nah-kah term-paht oon-tuk mer-nyey-wah ker-rey-tah*
I'd like...	**Saya ingin...** *sah-yah ee-ngin ...*
a cheap/small car	**sebuah kereta murah/kecil** *ser-boo-ah ker-rey-tah moo-rah/ker-chil*
an automatic/ a manual	**kereta automatik/manual** *ker-rey-tah ow-to-mah-tik/mah-noo-ahl*
air conditioning	**penyaman udara** *per-nyah-mahn oo-dah-rah*
a car seat	**tempat duduk kereta untuk budak** *term-paht doo-duk ker-rey-tah oon-tuk boo-dahk*
How much...?	**Berapakah...?** *ber-rah-pah-kah ...*
per day/week	**untuk sehari/seminggu** *oon-tuk ser-hah-ri/ ser-ming-goo*
per kilometer	**untuk sekilometer** *oon-tuk ser-ki-lo-mi-ter*
for unlimited mileage	**untuk perbatuan tanpa had** *oon-tuk per-bah-too-ahn tahn-pah hahd*
with insurance	**dengan insurans** *der-ngahn in-soo-rahns*
Are there any discounts?	**Ada diskaun?** *ah-dah dis-kown*

Roads are generally good except in parts of Sabah and Sarawak. The **North-South Expressway** that runs through Malaysia and links the south of Thailand with Singapore makes traveling by road much easier and faster. Car rentals are available for those who wish to self-drive.

You'll need an international driving licence or a valid licence from your own country. In most cases, drivers must be over 25. Cars are right-hand drive, and are driven on the left-hand side of the road.

The **Touch-n-Go** card is worth having so you can fly through the highway tolls. They can be purchased at toll booths en route.

YOU MAY HEAR...

Adakah anda ada lesen memandu antarabangsa?
ah-dah-kah ahn-dah ah-dah ley-sern mer-mahn-doo ahn-tah-rah-bahng-sah

Do you have an international driver's license?

Sila tunjukkan pasport anda.
si-lah toon-juk-kahn pas-port ahn-dah

Your passport, please.

Adakah anda ingin insurans?
ah-dah-kah ahn-dah ee-ngin in-soo-rahns

Do you want insurance?

Saya perlukan wang cagaran.
sah-yah per-loo-kahn wahng chah-gah-rahn

I'll need a deposit.

Tandatangan di sini.
tahn-dah-tah-ngahn di si-ni

Initial/Sign here.

Fuel Station

Where's the fuel station?	**Di mana stesen minyak?** *Di-mah-nah stey-seyn mee-nyahk*
Fill it up.	**Isikan sehingga penuh.** *ee-si-kahn ser-hing-gah per-nooh*
…Ringgit, please.	**…Ringgit, ya.** *Ring-git, yar.*
I'll pay in cash/ by credit card.	**Saya akan membayar dengan wang tunai/kad kredit.** *sah-yah ah-kahn bah-yar der-ngahn wahng too-nai/kahd kre-dit*

YOU MAY SEE…

GAS [PETROL]	gas [petrol]
BERPLUMBUM	leaded
TANPA PLUMBUM	unleaded
BIASA	regular
DIESEL	diesel
LAYAN DIRI	self-service
KHIDMAT PENUH	full-service

Asking Directions

Is this the way to…?	**Adakah ini arah ke…?**	*ah-dah-kah ee-ni ah-rah ker*
How far is it to…?	**Berapa jauh ke…?**	*ber-rah-pah jah-ooh ker…*
Where's…?	**Di manakah…?**	*di mah-nah-kah …*
…Street	**Jalan…**	*jah-lahn …*
this address	**alamat ini**	*ah-lah-maht ee-ni*
the highway [motorway]	**lebuhraya**	*ler-booh-rah-yah*

Can you show me on the map?	**Bolehkah anda tunjukkan di atas peta?** *bo-ley-kah ahn-dah toon-juk-kahn di ah-tahs per-tah*
I'm lost.	**Saya telah sesat.** *sah-yah ter-lah ser-saht*

YOU MAY HEAR…

terus ke hadapan *ter-roos ker hah-dah-pahn*	straight ahead
belok *bey-lok*	turn
kiri *ki-ri*	left
kanan *kah-nahn*	right
di/sebalik selekoh *di/ser-bah-lik ser-ley-koh*	on/around the corner
bertentangan *ber-tern-tah-ngahn*	opposite
belakang *ber-lah-kahng*	behind
sebelah *ser-ber-lah*	next to
selepas *ser-ler-pahs*	after
utara/selatan *oo-tah-rah/ser-lah-tahn*	north/south
timur/barat *ti-mur/bah-raht*	east/west
di lampu isyarat *di lahm-poo ee-siah-raht*	at the traffic light
di persimpangan jalan *di per-sim-pah-ngahn jah-lahn*	at the intersection

YOU MAY SEE...

 BERHENTI — stop

 BERI LALUAN — yield

 TIDAK BOLEH LETAK KENDERAAN — no parking

 SEHALA — one way

 TIDAK BOLEH MASUK — no entry

 KENDERAAN TIDAK DIBENARKAN — no vehicles allowed

 TIDAK BOLEH MEMOTONG — no passing

 ISYARAT LALU LINTAS DI HADAPAN — traffic signals ahead

KELUAR — exit

Parking

Can I park here?	**Bolehkah saya meletak kereta di sini?** *bo-ley-kah sah-yah mer-ler-tahk ker-rey-tah di si-ni*
Where's...?	**Di manakah...?** *di mah-nah-kah*
the parking garage	**tempat simpan kereta** *term-paht sim-pahn ker-rey-tah*
the parking lot [car park]	**tempat meletak kereta** *term-paht mer-ler-tahk ker-rey-tah*
the parking meter	**meter meletak kereta** *mi-ter mer-ler-tahk ker-rey-tah*

How much…?	**Berapakah harga…?** *ber-rah-pah-kah har-gah*
per hour	**untuk sejam** *oon-tuk ser-jahm*
per day	**untuk sehari** *oon-tuk ser-hah-ri*
for overnight	**untuk semalaman** *oon-tuk ser-mah-lahm-ahn*

Breakdown & Repair

My car broke down/ won't start.	**Kereta saya rosak/tidak boleh dihidupkan.** *ker-rey-tah sah-yah ro-sahk/ti-dahk bo-ley di-hi-doop-kahn*
Can you fix it (today)?	**Bolehkah anda memperbaikinya?** *bo-ley-kah ahn-dah merm-per-bai-ki-nyah*
When will it be ready?	**Bilakah ia akan siap?** *bi-lah-kah ee-ya ah-kahn see-yap*
How much?	**Berapakah harganya?** *ber-rah-pah-kah har-gah-nyah*

Accidents

| There was an accident. | **Ada kemalangan.** *ah-dah ker-mah-lahng-ahn* |
| Call an ambulance/ the police. | **Panggil ambulans/polis.** *pahng-gil ahm-boo-lahns/ po-lis* |

Places to Stay

ESSENTIAL

Can you recommend a hotel?	**Bolehkah anda mencadangkan sebuah hotel?** *bo-ley-kah ahn-dah mern-cha-dahng-kahn ser-buah ho-tel*
I have a reservation.	**Saya ada tempahan.** *sah-yah ah-da term-pah-han*
My name is...	**Nama saya ialah...** *nah-mah sah-yah ee-ya-lah*
Do you have a room...?	**Ada bilik...?** *ah-dah bi-lik*
for one/two	**untuk seorang/dua orang** *oon-tuk ser-o-rahng/ doo-ah o-rahng*
with a bathroom	**dengan bilik air** *der-ngahn bi-lik ah-er*
with air conditioning	**dengan penyaman udara** *der-ngahn per-nyah-mhan oo-dah-rah*
For...	**Untuk...** *oon-tuk*
tonight	**malam ini** *mah-lahm ee-ni*
two nights	**dua malam** *doo-ah mah-lahm*
one week	**seminggu** *ser-ming-goo*
How much?	**Berapakah harganya?** *ber-rah-pah-kah har-gah-nyah*
Is there anything cheaper?	**Adakah yang lebih murah?** *ah-dah-kah yahng ler-bih moo-rah*
When's checkout?	**Bilakah untuk mendaftar keluar?** *bi-lah-kah oon-tuk mern-dahf-tahr ker-loo-ah*
Can I leave this in the safe?	**Bolehkah saya menyimpan benda ini dalam peti keselamatan?** *bo-ley-kah sah-yah mer-nyim-pahn bern-dah ee-ni daj-lajm per-ti ker-ser-lah-mahh-than*
Can I leave my bags (here)?	**Bolehkah saya tinggalkan beg saya (di sini)?** *bo-ley-kah sah-yah ting-gahl-kahn beyg sah-yah (di si-ni)*

Can I have my bill/ a receipt?	**Bolehkah bagi saya bil/resit?** *bo-ley-kah bah-gi sah-yah bil/rer-sit*	
I'll pay in cash/ by credit card.	**Saya akan bayar dengan wang tunai/kad kredit.** *sah-yah ah-kahn bah-yar der-ngahn wahng too-nai/ kahd kre-dit*	

In Malaysia, accommodation ranges from five-star luxury hotels to the very basic **rumah tumpangan** (lodging house) and simple beach huts. The government regulates the industry by issuing licences to operate hotels and to sell alcohol. International hotels can be found in the state capitals and popular holiday spots. Two- or three-star hotels are usually decent, comfortable and safe, and many have air-conditioning.

Somewhere to Stay

Can you recommend…?	**Bolehkah anda mencadangkan…?** *bo-ley-kah ahn-dah mern-cha-dahng-kahn*
a hotel	**sebuah hotel** *ser-boo-ah ho-tel*
a hostel	**sebuah asrama** *ser-boo-ah ahs-rah-mah*
a campsite	**tapak perkhemahan** *tah-pahk per-kher-mah-han*
a bed and breakfast (B&B)	**penginapan dan sarapan** *per-ngi-nah-pahn dahn sar-rah-pahn*
What is it near?	**Dekat mana?** *der-kaht mah-nah*
How do I get there?	**Bagaimanakah saya pergi ke sana?** *bah-gai-mah-nah-kah sah-yah per-gi ker sah-nah*

At the Hotel

I have a reservation.	**Saya ada tempahan.**	*sah-yah ah-dah term-pah-han*
My name is...	**Nama saya ialah ...**	*nah-mah sah-yah ee-ya-lah ...*
Do you have a room...?	**Ada bilik ...?**	*ah-dah bi-lik ...*
with a toilet/ shower	**dengan bilik tandas/mandi hujan**	*der-ngahn bi-lik tahn-dahs/mahn-di hoo-jahn*
with air conditioning	**dengan penyaman udara**	*der-ngahn per-nyah-mahn oo-dah-rah*
that's smoking/ non-smoking	**yang dibenarkan merokok/dilarang merokok**	*yahng di-ber-nahr-kahn mer-ro-kok/di-lah-rahng mer-ro-kok*
For...	**Untuk...**	*oon-tuk ...*
tonight	**malam ini**	*mah-lahm ee-ni*
two nights	**dua malam**	*doo-ah mah-lahm*
a week	**seminggu**	*ser-ming-gu*
Do you have...?	**Adakah anda mempunyai ...?**	*ah-dah-kah ahn-dah merm-poo-nyah-i ...*
a computer	**sebuah komputer**	*ser-boo-ah kom-poo-ter*
an elevator [a lift]	**sebuah lif**	*ser-boo-ah lif*
(wireless) internet	**service perkhidmatan internet (tanpa wayar)**	*per-khid-mah-tahn in-ter-net (tahn-pah wah-yar)*

room service	**perkhidmatan bilik** *per-khid-mah-tahn bi-lik*
a pool	**sebuah kolam renang** *ser-boo-ah ko-lahm rer-nahng*
a gym	**sebuah gim** *ser-boo-ah jim*
I need…	**Saya perlu…** *sah-yah per-loo*
an extra bed	**sebuah katil tambahan** *ser-boo-ah kah-til tahm-bah-han*
a cot	**sebuah katil budak** *ser-boo-ah kah-til boo-dahk*
a crib	**sebuah katil bayi** *ser-boo-ah kah-til bah-yi*

For Numbers, see page 173.

YOU MAY HEAR…

Sila tunjukkan pasport/kad kredit anda. *si-lah toon-juk-kahn pas-port/ kad kre-dit ahn-dah*	Your passport/credit card, please.
Isikan borang ini. *ee-si-kahn bo-rahng ee-ni*	Fill out this form.
Tandatangan di sini. *tahn-dah-tah-ngahn di si-ni*	Sign here.

Price

How much per night/ week?	**Berapakah harga untuk semalam/seminggu?** *ber-rah-pah-kah har-gah oon-tuk ser-mah-lahm/ ser-ming-goo*
Does that include breakfast/tax?	**Adakah ia termasuk sarapan/cukai jualan?** *ah-dah-kah ee-ya ter-mah-suk sah-rah-pahn/chu-kai joo-ah-lahn*
Are there any discounts?	**Ada diskaun?** *ah-dah dis-kown*

Preferences

Can I see the room?	**Bolehkah saya melihat bilik?** *bo-ley-kah sah-yah mer-li-haht bi-lik*
I'd like a...room.	**Saya inginkan bilik yang...** *sah-yah ee-ngin-kahn bi-lik yahng ...*
better	**lebih baik** *ler-bih baik*
bigger	**lebih besar** *ler-bih ber-sahr*
cheaper	**lebih murah** *ler-bih moo-rah*
quieter	**lebih sunyi** *ler-bih soo-nyi*
I'll take it.	**Saya akan ambil bilik itu.** *sah-yah ah-kahn ahm-bil bi-lik ee-too*
No, I won't take it.	**Tidak, saya tidak mahu bilik itu.** *ti-dahk, sah-yah ti-dahk mah-hoo bi-lik ee-too*

Questions

Where is/are...?	**Di mana...?** *Di-mah-nah...*
the bar	**bar** *bar*
the bathrooms	**bilik mandi** *bi-lik mahn-di*
the elevator [lift]	**lif** *lif*
I'd like...	**Bolehkah bagi saya...?** *bo-ley-kah bah-gi sah-yah*
a blanket	**sehelai selimut** *ser-hi-lai ser-li-moot*
an iron	**sebuah seterika** *ser-boo-ah ser-ter-ri-kah*
the room key/key card	**kunci/kad kunci bilik.** *koon-chi/kahd koon-chi bi-lik*
a pillow	**sebuah bantal** *ser-boo-ah bahn-tahl*
soap	**sabun** *sah-boon*
toilet paper	**tisu tandas** *ti-soo tahn-dahs*
a towel	**sehelai tuala** *ser-hi-lai too-ah-lah*
Do you have an adapter for this?	**Adakah anda ada sebuah adaptor untuk alat ini?** *ah-dah-kah ahn-dah ah-dah ser-boo-ah ah-dahp-tor oon-tuk ah-laht ee-ni*

YOU MAY SEE...

TOLAK/TARIK	push/pull
BILIK AIR [TANDAS]	bathroom [toilet
BILIK MANDI HUJAN	shower
LIF	elevator [lift]
TANGGA	stairs
MESIN AIS	ice machines
MESIN LAYAN DIRI	vending machine
KAIN KOTOR	laundry
JANGAN GANGGU	do not disturb
PINTU API	fire door
PINTU KELUAR (KECEMASAN)	(emergency) exit
PANGGILAN BANGUN PAGI	wake-up call

How do you turn on the lights?	**Bagaimanakah saya memasangkan lampu?** *bah-gai-mah-nah-kah sah-yah mer-mah-sahng-kahn lahm-poo*
Can you wake me at…?	**Bolehkah anda bangunkan saya pada pukul…?** *bo-ley-kah ahn-dah bahn-goon-kahn sah-yah pah-dah poo-kool…*

Can I leave this in the safe?	**Bolehkah saya menyimpan benda ini dalam peti keselamatan?** *bo-ley-kah sah-yah mer-nyim-pahn bern-dah ee-ni dah-lahm per-ti ker-ser-lah-mah-tahn*
Can I have my things from the safe?	**Bolehkah saya dapatkan kembali barang-barang saya dari peti keselamatan?** *bo-ley-kah sah-yah dah-paht-kahn kerm-bah-li bah-rahng-bah-rahng sah-yah dah-ri per-ti ker-ser-lah-mah-tahn*
Is there mail/ a message for me?	**Ada mel/mesej untuk saya?** *ah-dah meyl/mey-seyj oon-tuk sah-yah*
Do you have a laundry service?	**Pukul berapakah anda tutup?** *pu-kul ber-ra-pa-kah aan-da tu-tup*

Problems

There's a problem.	**Ada masalah.** *ah-dah mah-sah-lah*
I lost my key/key card.	**Saya kehilangan kunci/kad kunci.** *sah-yah ker-hee-lah-ngahn koon-chi/kahd koon-chi*
I've locked my key/ key card in the room.	**Saya terkunci kunci/kad kunci dalam bilik.** *Sah-yah ter-kun-chi kadt kun-chi dah-lam bi-lik.*
There's no hot water/ toilet paper.	**Tidak ada air panas/tisu tandas.** *ti-dahk ah-dah ah-er pah-nahs/ti-soo tahn-dahs*
The room is dirty.	**Bilik ini kotor.** *bi-lik ee-ni ko-tor*

There are bugs in the room.	**Ada pepijat dalam bilik ini.** *ah-dah per-pi-jaht dah-lahm bi-lik ee-ni*
the air conditioning	**penyaman udara** *per-nyah-mahn oo-dah-rah*
the fan	**kipas** *ki-pahs*
the heat [heating]	**alat pemanas** *ah-laht per-mah-nahs*
the light	**lampu** *lahm-poo*
the TV	**televisyen** *tey-ley-vi-syen*
the toilet	**bilik air** *bi-lik ah-er*
…doesn't work.	**…tidak berfungsi.** *…ti-dahk ber-foong-si*
Can you fix…?	**Bolehkah anda baiki…?** *bo-ley-kah ahn-dah bai-ki*
I'd like another room.	**Saya ingin bilik yang lain.** *sah-yah ee-ngin bi-lik yahng lah-een*

The voltage used in Malaysia is 240 V. Outlets in Malaysia generally accept one type of plug, which comes with two parallel flat pins and a ground pin. You may need a converter and/or an adapter for your appliance.

Checking Out

When's check-out?	**Bilakah waktu mendaftar keluar?** *bi-lah-kah wahk-too mern-dahf-tahr ker-loo-ah*
Can I leave my bags here until…?	**Bolehkah saya tinggalkan beg saya di sini sehingga…?** *bo-ley-kah sah-yah ting-gahl-kahn beyg sah-yah di si-ni ser-hing-gah …*
Can I have an itemized bill/a receipt?	**Bolehkah bagi saya bil butiran/resit?** *bo-ley-kah bah-gi sah-yah bil boo-ti-rahn/rer-sit*
I think there's a mistake.	**Saya rasa ada kesilapan.** *sah-yah rah-sah ah-dah ker-si-lahp-ahn*
I'll pay in cash/ by credit card.	**Saya akan bayar dengan wang tunai/kad kredit.** *sah-yah ah-kahn bah-yar der-ngahn wahng too-nai/ kahd kre-dit*

Renting

I reserved an apartment/a room.	**Saya telah menempah sebuah apartmen/bilik.** *sah-yah ter-lah mer-nerm-pah ser-boo-ah ah-part-mern/bi-lik*
My name is…	**Nama saya ialah…** *nah-mah sah-yah ee-ya-lah*
Can I have the keys?	**Boleh saya dapatkan kunci?** *Bo-ley sah-yah dah-paht-kahn kun-chi?*
Are there…?	**Adakah…?** *ah-dah-kah*
dishes	**pinggan mangkuk** *ping-gahn mahng-kook*
pillows	**bantal** *bahn-tahl*
sheets	**cadar** *chah-dahr*
towels	**tuala** *too-ah-lah*
kitchen utensils	**perkakas dapur** *per-kah-kahs dah-poor*
When do I put out the bins /recycling?	**Bilakah saya perlu membawa keluar sampah/ barang-barang kitar semula?** *bi-lah-kah sah-yah per-loo merm-bah-wah ker-loo-ah sahm-pah/ bah-rahng-bah-rahng ki-tar ser-moo-lah*

…is broken.	**…ini sudah rosak** *ee-ni soo-dah ro-sahk*
How does… work?	**Macam mana…berfungsi?** *Mah-cham mah-nah… ber-fung-si?*
the air conditioner	**alat penyaman udara** *ah-laht per-nyah-mahn oo-dah-rah*
the dishwasher	**mesin basuh pinggan mangkuk** *mer-sin bah-sooh ping-gahn mahng-kook*
the freezer	**penyejuk beku** *per-nyey-jook ber-koo*
the microwave	**ketuhar gelombang** *ker-too-har ger-lom-bahng*
the refrigerator	**peti sejuk** *per-ti ser-jook*
the stove	**dapur** *dah-poor*
the washing machine	**mesin basuh** *mer-sin bah-sooh*

Domestic Items

I need…	**Saya perlu…** *sah-yah per-loo …*
an adapter	**sebuah adaptor** *ser-boo-ah ah-dahp-tor*
aluminum foil	**kerajang aluminium** *ker-rah-jahng ah-loo-mi-ni-ahm*
a bottle opener	**sebuah pembuka botol** *ser-boo-ah perm-boo-kah bo-tol*
a broom	**penyapu** *pern-nyah-poo*

a can opener	**sebuah pembuka tin**	*ser-boo-ah perm-boo-kah tin*
cleaning supplies	**bekalan bahan cuci**	*ber-kah-lahn bah-han choo-chi*
a corkscrew	**sebuah skru pencungkil gabus**	*ser-boo-ah skroo pern-chung-kil gah-boos*
detergent	**bahan cuci**	*bah-han choo-chi*
dishwashing liquid	**cecair mencuci pinggan mangkuk**	*cher-chah-er mern-choo-chi ping-gahn mahng-kook*
bin bags	**beg sampah**	*beyg sahm-pah*
a lightbulb	**sebiji mentol**	*ser-bi-ji mern-tol*
matches	**mancis**	*mahn-chis*
a mop	**mop**	*mop*
napkins	**napkin**	*napkin*
paper towels	**tisu tuala**	*ti-soo too-ah-lah*
plastic wrap [cling film]	**pembalut plastic**	*perm-bah-loot plahs-tik*
a plunger	**pelocok**	*per-lo-chok*
scissors	**gunting**	*goon-ting*
a vacuum cleaner	**sebuah pembersih hampagas**	*ser-boo-ah perm-ber-sih hahm-pah-gahs*

For Oven Temperatures, see page 179.

At the Hostel

Is there a bed available?	**Adakah anda mempunyai katil kosong?** *ah-dah-kah ahn-dah merm-poo-nyah-i kah-til ko-song*
I'd like...	**Saya mahu** *Sah-yah mah-hoo...*
a single/ double room	**sebuah bilik bujang/kelamin** *ser-boo-ah bi-lik boo-jahng/ker-lah-min*
a blanket	**sehelai selimut** *ser-hee-lai ser-li-moot*
a pillow	**sebuah bantal** *ser-boo-ah bahn-tahl*
sheets	**cadar** *chah-dar*
a towel	**sehelai tuala** *ser-hee-lai too-ah-lah*
Do you have lockers?	**Adakah anda mempunyai lokar?** *ah-dah-kah ahn-dah merm-poo-nyah-i lo-kar*
When do you lock up?	**Bilakah anda tutup?** *bi-lah-kah ahn-dah too-tup*
Do I need a membership card?	**Adakah saya perlu kad keahlian?** *ah-dah-kah sah-yah per-loo kahd ker-ah-li-ahn*
Here's my international student card.	**Ini ialah Kad Pelajar Antarabangsa saya.** *ee-ni ee-ya-lah kahd per-lah-jar ahn-tah-rah-bahng-sah sah-yah*

Malaysia does not have an extensive network of youth hostels, but what is available is adequate and clean. Hostels run by the **Malaysian Youth Hostels Association** can be found in KL, Malacca and Port Dickson. YMCAs can be found in Kuala Lumpur, Georgetown and Ipoh.

Budget chalets can be found along the east coast beaches, and on resort islands like Langkawi, Pangkor and Tioman.

Going Camping

Can I camp here?	**Bolehkah saya berkhemah di sini?** *bo-ley-kah sah-yah ber-kher-mah di si-ni*
Where's the campsite?	**Di manakah tapak perkhemahan?** *di mah-nah-kah tah-pak per-kher-mah-ahn*
What is the charge per day/week?	**Berapakah bayaran untuk sehari/seminggu?** *ber-rah-pah-kah bah-yar-ahn oon-tuk ser-hah-ri/ser-ming-goo*
Are there…?	**Adakah…?** *ah-dah-kah*
cooking facilities	**kemudahan memasak** *ker-moo-dah-han mer-mah-sahk*
electric outlets	**saluran tenaga elektrik** *sah-loo-rahn ter-nah-gah ee-leyk-trik*
laundry facilities	**kemudahan tempat mendobi** *ker-moo-dah-han term-paht mern-do-bi*
showers	**bilik mandi hujan** *bi-lik mahn-di hoo-jahn*
tents for hire	**khemah untuk disewa** *kher-mah oon-tuk di-sey-wah*
Where can I empty the chemical toilet?	**Di mana saya boleh kosongkan tandas kimia?** *Di-mah-nah sah-yah bo-ley koh-song-kahn than-das ki-mi-ah*

For Domestic Items, see page 49.

YOU MAY SEE…

AIR MINUMAN	drinking water
DILARANG BERKHEMAH	no camping
DILARANG MENYALAKAN API/ BERBARBEKU	no fires/barbecues

Communications

ESSENTIAL

Where's an internet cafe?	**Di manakah kafe internet?** *di mah-nah-kah kah-fey in-ter-net*
Can I access the internet/check my e-mail?	**Bolehkah saya melayari internet/memeriksa emel?** *bo-ley-kah sah-yah mer-lah-yah-ri in-ter-net/ mer-mer-rik-sah ee-meyl*
How much per half hour/hour?	**Berapakah bayaran untuk sejam (setengah jam)?** *ber-rah-pah-kah bah-yah-ran oon-tuk ser-jahm (ser-ter-ngah jahm)*
How do I connect/ log on?	**Bagaimanakah saya menyambung/log masuk ke internet?** *bah-gai-mah-nah-kah sah-yah mern-yahm-boong/log mah-suk ker in-ter-net*
A phone card, please.	**Sila berikan saya satu kad telefon.** *si-lah ber-ri-kahn sah-yah sah-too kahd tey-ley-fon*
Can I have your phone number?	**Bolehkah bagi saya nombor telefon anda?** *bo-ley-kah bah-gi sah-yah nom-bor tey-ley-fon ahn-da*
Here's my number/ e-mail.	**Ini ialah nombor telefon/alamat emel saya.** *ee-ni ee-ya-lah nom-bor tey-ley-fon/ah-lah-maht ee-meyl sah-yah*
Call/E-mail me.	**Panggil/Emel saya.** *pahng-gil/ee-meyl sah-yah*
Hello. This is...	**Helo. Ini ialah...** *hey-lo. ee-ni ee-ya-lah*
Can I speak to...?	**Boleh saya bercakap dengan...?** *bo-ley sah-yah ber-chah-kahp der-ngahn*
Can you repeat that?	**Bolehkah anda ulang semula?** *bo-ley-kah ahn-dah oo-lahng ser-moo-lah*
I'll call back later.	**Saya akan telefon kembali.** *Sah-yah ah-kahn tey-ley-fon kerm-bah-li*
Bye.	**Selamat tinggal.** *ser-lah-maht ting-gahl*

Where's the post office?	**Di manakah pejabat pos?** *di mah-nah-kah per-jah-baht pos*
I'd like to send this to…	**Saya ingin menghantar benda ini ke…** *sah-yah ee-ngin merng-hahn-tar bern-dah ee-ni ker*

Online

Where's an internet cafe?	**Di manakah kafe internet?** *di mah-nah-kah kah-fey in-ter-net*
Does it have wireless internet?	**Adakah ia mempunyai sambungan internet tanpa wayar?** *ah-dah-kah ee-ya merm-poo-nyah-i sahm-boo-ngahn in-ter-net tahn-pah wah-yar*
What is the WiFi password?	**Apa kata laluan WiFi** *Ah-pah kah-tah lah-loo-ahn WiFi*
Is the WiFi free?	**WiFi percuma ke?** *WiFi Per-choo-mah ker?*
Do you have bluetooth?	**Awak ada Bluetooth?** *Ah-wahk ah-dah Bluetooth?*
Can you show me how to turn on/off the computer?	**Bagaimanakah saya memasang/menutup komputer ini?** *bah-gai-mah-nah-kah sah-yah mer-mah-sahng/mer-noo-toop kom-poo-ter ee-ni*
Can I…?	**Bolehkah saya…?** *bo-ley-kah sah-yah*
access the internet	**melayari internet** *mer-lah-yah-ri in-ter-net*
check my e-mail	**memeriksa emel** *mer-mer-rik-sah ee-meyl*
print	**mencetak** *mern-cher-tahk*
plug in/charge my laptop/iPhone/iPad/BlackBerry?	**Pasang/cas komputer riba/iPhone/iPad/BlackBerry saya?** *Pah-sahng kom-pu-ter ri-bah iPhone/iPad/BlackBerry sah-yah*
access Skype?	**Guna Skype?** *Goo-nah Skype*
How much per half hour/hour?	**Berapa untuk setengah jam/sejam?** *ber-rah-pah oon-tuk Ser-teer-ngah jahm/ser-jahm*

How do I...?	**Bagaimanakah saya ...?** *bah-gai-mah-nah-kah* *sah-yah*
connect/disconnect	**menyambung/memutuskan sambungan** *mern-nyahm-boong/mer-moo-toos-kahn* *sahm-boo-ngahn*
log on/off	**log masuk/log keluar** *log mah-suk/log ker-loo-ah*
type this symbol	**menaip simbol ini** *mer-naip sim-bol ee-ni*
What's your e-mail?	**Apakah alamat emel anda?** *ah-pah-kah* *ah-lah-maht ee-meyl ahn-dah*
My e-mail is...	**Alamat emel saya ialah...** *ah-lah-maht ee-meyl* *sah-yah ee-ya-lah*
Do you have a scanner?	**Awak ada pengimbas?** *Ah-wak ah-dah* *per-nghim-bas*

Internet cafes and Wi-fi broadband services can be found in all
the major cities and tourist areas. Pre-paid internet starter packs
are also available from major telecommunications providers such as
Maxis, **DiGI** and **Celecom**.

Social Media

Are you on Facebook/Twitter?	**Awak ada Facebook/Twitter?** *Ah-wak ah-dah Facebook/Twitter*
What's your user name?	**Apa nama pengguna awak?** *Ah-pah nah-mah peng-goo-nah ah-wak*
I'll add you as a friend.	**Saya akan tambah awak sebagai kawan.** *Sah-yah ah-kahn tahm-bah ah-wak ser-bah-gai kah-wahn*
I'll follow you on Twitter.	**Saya akan ikuti awak di Twitter.** *Sah-yah ah-kahn i-koo-ti ah-wak di Twitter*
Are you following…?	**Awak ada ikuti…?** *Ah-wak ah-dah i-koo-ti…*
I'll put the pictures on Facebook/Twitter.	**Saya akan letak gambar di Facebook/Twitter.** *Sah-yah ah-kahn ler-tak gam-bar di Facebook/Twitter*

YOU MAY SEE…

TUTUP	close
PADAM	delete
EMEL	e-mail
KELUAR	exit
BANTUAN	help
PESANAN SEGERA	instant messenger
INTERNET	internet
LOG MASUK	login
(MESEJ) BARU	new (message)
PASANG/TUTUP	on/off
BUKA	open
CETAK	print
SIMPAN	save
HANTAR	send
ID PENGGUNA/KATA LALUAN	username/password
INTERNET TANPA WAYAR	wireless internet

| I'll tag you in the pictures. | **Saya akan tanda awak dalam gambar.** *Sah-yah ah-kahn than-dah ah-wak dah-lamn gam-bar* |

Phone

A phone card/prepaid phone, please.	**Sila berikan saya kad telefon/kad telefon prabayar.** *si-lah ber-ri-kahn sah-yah kahd tey-ley-fon/kahd tey-ley-fon prah-bah-yar*
How much?	**Berapakah harganya?** *ber-rah-pah-kah har-gah-nyah*
What's the area country code for…?	**Apakah kod kawasan/negara untuk…?** *ah-pah-kah kod kah-wah-sahn/ner-gah-rah oon-tuk*
What's the number for Information?	**Apakah nombor untuk Keterangan?** *ah-pah-kah nom-bor oon-tuk ker-ter-rah-ngahn*
I'd like the number for…	**Saya nak nombor untuk…** *sah-yah nahk nom-bor oon-tuk…*
I'd like to call collect [reverse the charges].	**Saya nak buat panggilan caj balikan.** *sah-yah nahk boo-art pahng-gi-lahn carj bah-li-kahn*
My phone doesn't work here.	**Telefon saya tidak berfungsi di sini.** *tey-ley-fon sah-yah ti-dahk ber-foong-si di si-ni*
What network are you on?	**Awak guna rangkaian apa?** *ah-wahk goo-nah rahng-kah-yahn ah-pah*
Is it 3G?	**3G ke?** *3G ker*

I have run out of credit/minutes.	**Saya dah habis kredit/masa.** *sah-yah dah hah-bis kre-dit/mah-sah*
Can I buy some credit?	**Boleh saya beli kredit?** *Bo-ley sah-yah sah-yah ber-li kre-dit*
Do you have a phone charger?	**Awak ada pengecas telefon?** *ah-wahk ah-dah per-nger-cas tey-ley-fon*
Can I have your number?	**Boleh saya dapatkan nombor awak?** *Bo-ley sah-yah dah-pat-kahn nom-bor ah-wahk*
Here's my number.	**Ini nombor saya.** *ee-ni nom-bor sah-yah*
Please call/text me.	**Sila telefon/sms saya.** *Si-lah tey-ley-fon/sms sah-yah*
I'll call/text you.	**Saya akan telefon/sms awak.** *Sah-yah ah-kahn tey-ley-fon/ sms ah-wahk*

For Numbers, see page 173.

Telephone Etiquette

Hello. This is…	**Hai. Saya…** *Hi. Sah-yah*
Can I speak to…?	**Boleh saya bercakap dengan…?** *Bo-ley sah-yah ber-cah-kap der-ngahn…*
Extension…	**Sambungan…** *Sahm-boo-ngahn…*
Speak louder/more slowly, please.	**Tolong cakap kuat/perlahan sikit.** *Toh-long cah-kahp koo-aht/per-lah-hahn see-kit*
Can you repeat that?	**Boleh awak ulang semula?** *Bo-ley ah-wahk oo-lang ser-moo-lah*
I'll call back later.	**Nanti saya telefon balik.** *Nahn-ti sah-yah tey-ley-fon bah-lik*
Bye.	**Terima kasih.** *Ter-ri-mah Kah-sih*

For Business Travel, see page 145.

You may have noticed that the actual translation for 'bye' or 'good bye' is **selamat tinggal** (see inside front cover). However, when speaking on the phone, you should use **Terima Kasih**, meaning 'thank you'.

YOU MAY HEAR...

Siapa yang panggil?
siah-pah yahng pahng-gil

Who's calling?

Tunggu sebentar. *toong-goo ser-bern-tar*

Hold on.

Saya akan menyambungkan anda. *sah-yah ah-kahn mer-nyahm-boong-kahn ahn-dah*

I'll put you through.

Dia tidak ada di sini/di talian yang lain.
di-ah ti-dahk ah-dah di si-ni/di tah-lee-yan yahng lah-een

He/She is not here/ on another line.

Adakah anda ingin meninggalkan mesej?
ah-dah-kah ahn-dah ee-ngin mer-ning-gahl-kahn mey-seyj

Would you like to leave a message?

Panggil semula nanti/ dalam 10 minit.
pahng-gil ser-moo-lah nahn-ti/dah-lahm 10 mi-nit

Call back later/ in 10 minutes.

Bolehkah dia memanggil anda semula?
bo-ley-kah di-ah mer-mahng-gil ahn-dah ser-moo-lah

Can he/she call you back?

Apakah nombor anda?
ah-pah-kah nom-bor ahn-dah

What's your number?

Fax

Can I send/receive a fax here?	**Bolehkah saya menghantar/menerima fax di sini?** *bo-ley-kah sah-yah merng-hahn-tar/ mer-ner-ri-mah fax di si-ni*
What's the fax number?	**Apakah nombor fax di sini?** *ah-pah-kah nom-bor fax di si-ni*
Please fax this to...	**Sila hantarkan fax ini ke...** *si-lah hahn-tar-kahn fax ee-ni ker...*

Post

Where's the post office/mailbox?	**Di manakah pejabat pos/peti surat?** *di mah-nah-kah per-jah-baht pos/per-ti soo-raht*
A stamp for this postcard/letter to...	**Sekeping setem untuk poskad/surat ini untuk dihantar kepada...** *ser-ker-ping ser-term oon-tuk pos-kahd/soo-raht ee-ni oon-tuk di-hahn-tar ker-pah-dah*
How much?	**Berapakah harganya?** *ber-rah-pah-kah har-gah-nyah*
Send this package by airmail/express.	**Hantarkan pakej ini denganmel udara/pos laju.** *hahn-tar-kahn pah-keyj ee-ni der-ngahn mely oo-dah-rah/pos lah-joo*
A receipt, please.	**Sila berikan saya resit.** *si-lah ber-ri-kahn sah-yah rer-sit*

YOU MAY HEAR...

Isikan borang pengisytiharan kastam.
ee-si-kahn bo-rahng per-ngi-si-ti-hah-rahn kahs-tahm

Fill out the customs declaration form.

Apakah nilai benda ini?
ah-pah-kah ni-lai bern-dah ee-ni

What's the value?

Apakah yang ada di dalam?
ah-pah-kah yahng ah-dah di dah-lahm

What's inside?

The Malaysian postal service (**www.pos.com.my**) is reliable, and there are post offices everywhere. They are generally open Monday to Friday between 8:00a.m. and 5:00p.m. Stamped items can go directly into the red post boxes scattered about. Stamps and aerogrammes are often sold at small Indian sweet and tobacco stalls on street corners.

Food & Drink

ESSENTIAL

Can you recommend a good restaurant/ bar?	**Bolehkah anda mencadangkan sebuah bagus?** *bo-ley-kah ahn-dah mern-chah-dahng-kahn ser-boo-ah reys-to-rahn/bahr yahng bah-goos*
Is there a Malay/ inexpensive restaurant nearby?	**Adakah restoran berdekatan sini?** *ah-dah-kah reys-to-rahn mah-kahn-ahn Mer-lah-yoo/ koo-rahng mah-hal ber-der-kaht-ahn si-ni*
A table for…, please.	**Sila berikan meja untuk…** *si-lah ber-ri-kahn mey-jah oon-tuk …*
Can we sit…?	**Bolehkah kami duduk…?** *bo-ley-kah kah-mi doo-duk …*
here/there	**di sini/di sana** *di si-ni/di sah-nah*
outside	**di luar** *di loo-ah*
in a non-smoking area	**di kawasan dilarang merokok** *di kah-wah-sahn di-lah-rahng mer-ro-kok*
I'm waiting for someone.	**Saya sedang menunggu seseorang** *sah-yah ser-dahng mer-noong-goo ser-ser-o-rahng*
Where's the restroom [toilet]?	**Di manakah bilik air?** *di mah-nah-kah bi-lik ah-er*
A menu, please.	**Sila berikan menu.** *si-lah ber-ri-kahn mey-noo*
What do you recommend?	**Apakah yang anda cadangkan?** *ah-pah-kah yahng ahn-dah chah-dahng-kahn*
I'd like…	**Saya inginkan…** *sah-yah ee-ngin-kahn*
Some more…, please.	**Sila berikan lebih** *si-lah ber-ri-kahn ler-bih*
Enjoy your meal!	**Nikmatilah hidangan anda.** *nik-mah-ti-lah hi-dah-ngahn ahn-dah*

The check [bill], please.	**Sila berikan bil** *si-lah ber-ri-kahn bil*
Is service included?	**Adakah ini termasuk caj perkhidmatan?**
	ah-dah-kah ee-ni ter-mah-suk chaj per-khid-mah-than
Can I pay by credit card/have a receipt?	**Bolehkah saya?** *bo-ley-kah sah-yah bah-yah*
	der-ngahn kahd krey-dit/dah-paht-kahn rey-sit
Thank you!	**Terima kasih!** *ter-ri-mah kah-sih*

Where to Eat

Can you recommend...?	**Bolehkah anda mencadangkan**
	bo-ley-kah ahn-dah mern-chah-dahng-kahn
a restaurant	**sebuah restoran** *ser-boo-ah reys-to-rahn*
a bar	**sebuah bar** *ser-boo-ah bahr*
a café	**sebuah kafe** *ser-boo-ah kah-fey*
a fast food place	**sebuah restoran makanan segera** *ser-boo-ah reys-to-rahn mah-kahn-ahn*
a cheap restaurant	**restoran murah** *reys-to-rahn moo-rah*
an expensive restaurant	**restoran mahal** *reys-to-rahn mah-hal*
a restaurant with a good view	**restoran dengan pemandangan cantik**
	reys-to-rahn der-ngahn per-mahn-dah-ngahn cahn-tik
an authentic/ a non-touristy restaurant	**restoran autentik/bukan untuk pelancong**
	reys-to-rahn au-tehn-tik/buh-kahn oon-tuk per-lahn-coong

Reservations & Preferences

I'd like to reserve a table...	**Saya ingin menempah sebuah meja...**
	sah-yah ee-ngin mer-nerm-pah ser-boo-ah mey-jah ...
for two	**untuk dua orang** *oon-tuk doo-ah o-rahng*
for this evening	**untuk petang ini** *oon-tuk per-tahng ee-ni*

YOU MAY HEAR...

Adakah anda membuat tempahan?
ah-dah-kah ahn-dah merm-boo-aht term-pah-han

Do you have a reservation?

Berapa orang? *ber-rah-pah o-rahng*

How many?

Tempat merokok atau tempat dilarang merokok? *term-paht mer-ro-kok ah-tow term-paht di-lah-rahng mer-ro-kok*

Smoking or non-smoking?

Adakah anda telah bersedia untuk memesan (makanan)? *ah-dah-kah ahn-dah ter-lah ber-ser-dee-ya oon-tuk mer-mer-sahn (mah-kah-nahn)*

Are you ready (to order)?

Apakah yang anda mahu?
ah-pah-kah yahng ahn-dah mow

What would you like?

Saya mencadangkan
sah-yah mern-chah-dahng-kahn

I recommend...

Nikmatilah hidangan anda
nik-mah-tilah hi-dahn-gan ahn-dah

Enjoy your meal.

for tomorrow at…	**untuk esok pada pukul…** *oon-tuk ey-sok pah-dah poo-kool …*
A table for two, please.	**Sila berikan meja untuk dua orang.** *si-lah ber-ri-kahn mey-jah oon-tuk doo-ah o-rahng*
I have a reservation.	**Kami ada tempahan** *kah-mi ah-dah term-pah-hahn*
My name is…	**Nama saya ialah…** *nah-mah sah-yah ee-ya-lah …*
Can we sit…?	**Bolehkah kami duduk…?** *bo-ley-kah kah-mi doo-duk*
here/there	**di sini/di sana** *di si-ni/di sah-nah*
outside	**di luar** *di loo-ah*
in a non smoking area	**di kawasan dilarang merokok** *di kah-wah-sahn di-lah-rahng mer-ro-kok*
by the window	**berdekatan tingkap** *ber-der-kaht-ahn ting-kahp*
in the shade	**di tempat redup** *di-tem-paht rer-doop*
in the sun	**di tempat panas** *di-tem-paht pah-nas*
Where are the toilets?	**Di manakah bilik air?** *di mah-nah-kah bi-lik ah-er*

How to Order

Excuse me, sir/ma'am?	**Pelayan!** *per-lah-yahn*
We're ready (to order).	**Kita sudah bersedia untuk memesan (makanan)** *ki-tah soo-dah ber-ser-dee-ya oon-tuk mer-mer-sahn (mah-kah-nahn)*
The wine list, please.	**Sila berikan senarai wain** *si-lah ber-ri-kahn ser-nah-rai wain*
I'd like…	**Saya inginkan…** *sah-yah ee-ngin-kahn …*
a bottle of…	**sebotol…** *ser-bo-tol*
a carafe of…	**satu serahi…** *sah-too ser-rah-hee …*
a glass of…	**segelas…** *ser-ger-lahs …*
The menu, please.	**Sila berikan menu.** *si-lah ber-ri-kahn mey-noo*
Do you have…?	**Adakah anda mempunyai…?** *ah-dah-kah ahn-dah merm-poon-ya*
a menu in English	**menu dalam Bahasa Inggeris** *mey-noo dah-lahm*

Bah-hah-sah Ing-ger-ris

a fixed price menu	**menu harga tetap** *mey-noo har-gah ter-tahp*	
a children's menu	**menu untuk kanak-kanak** *mey-noo oon-tuk kah-nahk-kah-nahk*	

What do you recommend?	**Apakah yang anda cadangkan?** *ah-pah-kah yahng ahn-dah chah-dahng-kahn*	
What's this?	**Apakah ini?** *ah-pah-kah ee-ni*	
What's in it?	**Apakah yang ada di dalam?** *ah-pah-kah yahng ah-dah di dah-lahm*	
Is it spicy?	**Adakah ia pedas?** *ah-dah-kah ee-ya per-dahs*	
Without…, please.	**Sila berikan tanpa…** *si-lah ber-ri-kahn tahn-pah …*	
It's to go [take away].	**Bungkuskan.** *boong-koos-kahn*	

For Drinks, see page 83.

YOU MAY SEE…

CAJ MASUK	cover charge
HARGA TETAP	fixed price
MENU HARI INI	menu (of the day)
TAK TERMASUK KHIDMAT	service (not) included
ISTIMEWA	specials

Cooking Methods

baked	**dibakar** *di-bah-kar*
barbecued	**panggang** *pahng-gang*
boiled	**direbus** *di-rer-boos*
braised	**ditumis-reneh** *di-too-mis-rey-neyh*
breaded	**disalut dengan serbuk roti** *di-sah-loot der-ngahn ser-book ro-ti*
creamed	**berkrim** *ber-krim*

diced	**dipotong dadu**	di-po-tong dah-doo
filleted	**dipotong dengan membuang tulang**	di-po-tong der-ngahn merm-boo-ahng too-lahng
fried/ deep-fried	**digoreng**	di-go-reyng
grilled	**dipanggang**	di-pahng-gahng
poached	**direneh**	di-rey-neyh
roasted	**dipanggang**	di-pahng-gahng
sautéed	**dimasak secara sauté**	di-mah-sahk ser-chah-rah sau-te
smoked	**disalai**	di-sah-lai
steamed	**dikukus**	di-koo-koos
stewed	**dimasak secara merendidih**	di-mah-sahk ser-chah-rah mer-ren-di-dih
stir-fried	**digoreng kilas**	di-goh-reyng key-las
stuffed	**disumbat dengan isi ramuan**	di-soom-baht der-ngahn ee-si rah-moo-ahn

Dietary Requirements

I'm...	**Saya...**	sah-yah
diabetic	**menghidap diabetes**	merng-hi-dahp dia-bey-teys
lactose intolerant	**menghidap penyakit kurang upaya memproses laktosa**	merng-hi-dahp pern-yahkit koo-rahng oo-pah yah merm-pro-seys lahk-to-sah
vegetarian	**vegetarian**	veg-et-tare-ee-an
vegan	**vegan**	vee-gahn
I'm allergic to...	**Saya alah kepada**	sah-yah ah-lah ker-pah-dah
I can't eat...	**Saya tidak boleh makan**	sah-yah ti-dahk bo-ley mah-kahn
dairy products	**hasil tenusu**	hah-sil ter-noo-soo
gluten	**gluten**	gloo-teyn
nuts	**kacang**	kah-chahng
pork	**daging babi**	dah-ging bah-bi

shellfish	**kerang-kerangan**	*ker-rahng-ker-rahng-ngahn*
spicy foods	**kerang-kerangan**	*ker-rahng-ker-rahng-ngahn*
wheat	**gandum**	*gahn-doom*
Is it halal/kosher?	**Adakah ia halal?**	*ah-dah-kah ee-ya hah-lahl*
Do you have…?	**Awak ada…?**	*Ah-wakh ah-dah*
skimmed milk	**susu tanpa lemak**	*soo-soo tahn-pah ler-makh*
whole milk	**susu penuh**	*soo-soo peh-nuh*
soya milk	**susu soya**	*soo-soo soh-yah*

Dining with Children

Do you have children's portions?	**Adakah anda mempunyai hidangan saiz kanak-kanak?** *ah-dah-kah ahn-dah merm-poon-yai hi-dah-ngahn sah-iz kah-nahk-kah-nahk*
A highchair/child's seat, please.	**Sila berikan kerusi tinggi budak** *si-lah ber-ri-kahn ker-roo-si ting-gi boo-dahk*
Where can I feed/ change the baby?	**Di manakah saya boleh menyusu bayi?** *di mah-nah-kah sah-yah bo-ley mern-yoo-soo bah-yi*
Can you warm this?	**Bolehkah anda panaskan yang ini kepada suhu yang suam?** *bo-ley-kah ahn-dah pah-nahs-kahn yahng ee-ni ker-pah-dah soo-hoo yahng soo-ahm*

For Traveling with Children, see page 148.

How to Complain

When will our food be ready?	**Berapa lama lagi perlu kami tunggu sebelum makanan dihidang?** *ber-rah-pah lah-mah lah-gi per-loo kah-mi toong-goo ser-ber-loom mah-kah-nahn di-hi-dahng*
We can't wait any longer.	**Kita tidak boleh tunggu lagi.** *ki-tah ti-dahk bo-ley toong-goo lah-gi*
We're leaving.	**Kita akan meninggalkan** *ki-tah ah-kahn mer-ning-gahl-kahn (term-paht ee-ni)*
I didn't order this.	**Saya tidak memesan ini.** *sah-yah ti-dahk mer-mer-sahn (mah-kah-nahn) ee-ni*
I ordered…	**Saya memesan** *sah-yah mer-mer-sahn*
I can't eat this.	**Saya tidak boleh makan ini.** *sah-yah ti-dahk bo-ley mah-kahn (mah-kah-nahn) ee-ni*
This is too…	**Ini terlalu…** *(mah-kah-nan) ee-ni ter-lah-loo*
cold/hot	**sejuk/panas** *ser-jook/pah-nahs*
salty/spicy	**masin/pedas** *mah-sin/per-dahs*
tough/bland	**liat/tawar** *li-aht/tah-wahr*
This isn't clean/fresh.	**Ini tidak** *ee-ni ti-dahk ber-sih/ser-gar*

Paying

The check [bill], please.	**Sila berikan bil.** *si-lah ber-ri-kahn bil*
Separate checks [bills], please.	**Sila asingkan bil.** *si-lah ah-sing-kahn bil*
It's all together.	**Semua sekali.** *ser-moo-ah ser-kah-li*
Is service included?	**Adakah ia termasuk caj perkhidmatan?** *ah-dah-kah ee-ya ter-mah-suk chaj per-khid-maht-tahn*
What's this amount for?	**Jumlah ini untuk apa?** *joom-lah ee-ni oon-tuk ah-pah*

I didn't have that.	**Saya tidak makan yang itu. Saya makan…**
I had…	*sah-yah ti-dahk mah-kahn yahng ee-too. sah-yah*
	mah-kahn…
Can I have a receipt/	**Bolehkah bagi saya resit/bil butiran?** *bo-ley-kah*
an itemized bill?	*bah-gi sah-yah rer-sit/bil boo-ti-rahn*
That was delicious!	**Sedapnya!** *ser-dahp-nyah*
I've already paid.	**Saya sudah bayar.** *Sah-yah soo-dah bah-yar*

In most hotels and large restaurants, a 10 per cent government tax and 5 per cent service tax is added to the bill, so tipping is not obligatory. However, it is appreciated and can be common, but only in the cities and major tourist spots. In some restaurants, you can just leave behind the loose change. Tourist guides expect a tip. Otherwise, a simple **terima kasih** (thank you) and a smile will do.

Meals & Cooking

Meals & Cooking

In Malaysia, ethnic, regional and religious influences play a determining role in the ingredients used and how dishes are prepared. Halal restaurants follow strict Muslim dietary regulations and do not serve pork or alcohol. In Melaka and Penang, Peranakan (or Nonya) cuisine combines Chinese and Malay styles and includes dishes such as **kari kapitan** (curry chicken) and **otak-otak** (fishcake with spices steamed in banana leaf). Authentic Malay dishes including rice and fish dishes such as **nasi dagang** and barbecued chicken (**ayam percik**) can be found on the east coast in states such as Kelantan and Terengganu. Meanwhile, Sarawak has its own specialities again, featuring Malay, Indian, Chinese and Dayak influences. The spicy Sarawak **laksa** is a big favourite, as is **umei**, a Melanau dish of raw fish marinated with chilli, lime and shallots. Fresh seafood, venison, wild boar, **pansoh manok** (an iban chicken dish cooked in bamboo tubes with rice wine) are not to be missed.

Breakfast

Bacon	**bacon** *bak-on*
butter	**mentega** *mern-tey-gah*
coffee/tea...	**kopi/teh** *ko-pi/tey*
black	**hitam** *hi-tahm*
decaf	**tanpa kafein** *tahn-pah kah-fey-in*
with milk	**dengan susu** *der-ngah soo-soo*
with sugar	**dengan gula** *der-ngah goo-lah*
with artificial	**dengan pemanis tiruan** *der-ngah per-mah-nis*
sweetener	*ti-roo-ahn*
cold/hot cereal	**bijirin sejuk/panas** *bih-jih-rin ser-jook/pah-nas*
cold cuts	**hirisan daging masak sejuk** *hi-ri-sahn dah-gihng*
	mah-sak ser-jook
croissant	**croissant** *krwah-sawn*
jam/jelly	**jem/jeli** *jam/ jelly*
cheese	**keju** *key-joo*
... juice	**jus...** *joos*
orange	**oren** *o-reyn*
apple	**epal** *ey-pahl*
grapefruit	**limau gedang** *li-mow ger-dahng*
milk	**susu** *soo-soo*
oatmeal	**bubur oat** *boo-boor oat*
water	**air** *ah-er*
granola [muesli]	**granola [muesli] campuran bijiran** *cham-poo-rahn*
	bi-ji-rahn
muffin	**muffin** *(same as English pronunciation)*
... egg	**telur** *ter-loor*
hard /soft boiled	**rebus/setengah masak** *rer-boos/ser-tern-gah*
	mah-sahk
fried	**goreng** *go-reyng*
scrambled	**hancur** *hahn-coor*

omelet	**telur dadar** *dah-dar*
bread	**roti** *ro-ti*
toast	**roti bakar** *ro-ti bah-kar*
roll	**gulung** *gooh-long*
sausage	**sosej** *so-seyj*
yogurt	**yogurt** *yogurt*

Appetizers

...soup	**Sup ...** *soop*
chicken	**ayam** *ah-yahm*
meat, seafood and egg	**daging, makanan laut dan telur** *dah-ging, mah-kahn-ahn lah-oot dahn ter-loor*
pork	**daging babi** *dah-ging bah-bi*
lamb	**daging kambing** *dah-ging kahm-bing*
oxtail	**ekor lembu** *ey-kor lerm-boo*
seafood	**makanan laut** *mah-kah-nahn lah-oot*
spare rib	**tulang rusuk** *too-lahng roo-suk*
squid	**sotong** *so-tong*
tomato	**tomato** *to-mah-to*
vegetable	**sayur-sayuran** *sah-yoor-sah-yoor-rahn*

Malaysia offers a wide range of food choices, ranging from fine dining to street food. Breakfast is usually available from 6:00 to 10:30 a.m., and lunch carries on from noon or just before until 2:00p.m. Dinner is served from 6:30p.m. until 11:00p.m. Outside of these hours, you will also find stalls and restaurants that serve food all day.

Fish & Seafood

carp	**ikan kap**	*ee-kahn kahp*
clam	**kepah/kima**	*ker-pah/ki-mah*
cod	**ikan kod**	*ee-kahn kod*
crab	**ketam**	*ker-tahm*
halibut	**halibut**	*hah-li-boot*
herring	**ikan hering**	*ee-kahn her-ring*
lobster	**udang galah**	*oo-dahng gah-lah*
octopus	**sotong kurita**	*so-tong koo-ri-tah*
oyster	**tiram**	*ti-rahm*
salmon	**ikan salmon**	*ee-kahn sahl-mon*
salted fish	**ikan masin**	*ee-kahn mah-sin*
sea bass	**ikan bes laut**	*ee-kahn beys lah-oot*
shrimp	**udang**	*oo-dahng*
sole	**ikan sisa Nabi**	*ee-kahn si-sah nah-bi*
squid	**sotong**	*so-tong*
swordfish	**ikan todak**	*ee-kahn to-dahk*
trout	**ikan trout**	*ee-kahn trout*
tuna	**ikan tuna**	*ee-kahn tuna*

Meat & Poultry

barbecued pork	**daging babi salai**	*dah-ging bah-bi sah-lai*
beef	**daging lembu**	*dah-ging lerm-boo*
chicken	**ayam**	*ah-yahm*
duck	**itik**	*ee-tik*
ham	**ham**	*ham*
lamb	**daging kambing**	*dah-ging kahm-bing*
liver	**hati**	*hah-ti*
oxen entrails	**organ dalaman lembu jantan**	
	or-gahn dah-lahm-ahn lerm-boo jahn-tahn	
pork	**daging babi**	*dah-ging bah-bi*
sausage	**sosej**	*so-seyj*
spare ribs	**tulang rusuk**	*too-lahng roo-suk*
steak	**stik**	*stik*
veal	**daging anak lembu**	*dah-ging a-nak lerm-bu*
oxen tripe	**perut lembu**	*per-rut lerm-bu*

Vegetables & Staples

asparagus	**pucuk asparagus**	*poo-chook ahs-pah-rah-goos*
broccoli	**brokoli**	*bro-ko-li*
cabbage	**kubis**	*koo-bis*

capsicum	**lada benggala** *lah-dah berng-gah-lah*
carrot	**lobak merah** *lo-bahk mey-rah*
cauliflower	**kubis bunga** *koo-bis boo-ngah*
celery	**daun saderi** *dah-oon sah-der-ri*
Chinese cabbage	**kubis cina** *koo-bis chi-nah*
Corn	**jagung** *jah-goong*
Curryleaves	**daun kari** *dah-oon kah-ri*
Longbean	**kacang panjang** *kah-chahng pahn-jahng*
eggplant [aubergine]	**terung ungu** *ter-roong oo-ngoo*
garlic	**bawang putih** *bah-wahng poo-tih*
green bean	**kacang hijau** *kah-chahng hee-jow*
lemongrass	**serai** *ser-rai*
lettuce	**selada** *ser-lah-dah*
mushroom	**cendawan** *chern-dah-wahn*
olive	**buah zaitun** *boo-ah zai-toon*
okra [lady's finger]	**bendi** *beyn-di*
scallion [spring onion]	**daun bawang** *dah-oon bah-wahng*
noodles	**mee** *mee*
pea	**kacang pis** *kah-chahng pis*
potato	**ubi kentang** *oo-bi kern-tahng*
radish	**lobak putih** *lo-bahk poo-tih*
rice	**nasi** *nah-si*
red/green pepper	**lada merah/hijau** *lah-dah mey-rah/hee-jow*
seaweed	**rumpai laut** *room-pai lah-oot*
soy bean	**kacang soya** *kah-chahng so-yah*
spinach	**bayam** *bah-yahm*
tofu	**tauhu** *tow-hoo*
tomato	**tomato** *to-mag-to*
vegetable	**sayur-sayuran** *sah-yoor-sah-yoor-ahn*
zucchini	**zukini** *zoo-ki-ni*

Fruit

apple	**epal** *ey-pahl*
banana	**pisang** *pi-sahng*
carambola [starfruit]	**belimbing** *ber-lim-bing*
chiku	**ciku** *chi-koo*
custardapple	**buah nona** *boo-ah no-nah*
coconut	**kelapa** *ker-lah-pah*
dates	**kurma** *kur-mah*
mandarin orange	**limau mandarin** *li-mow mahn-dah-rin*
mangosteen	**manggis** *mahng-gis*
fruits	**buah-buahan** *boo-ah-boo-ah-hahn*
grapefruit	**limau gedang [limau besar]** *li-mow ger-dahng [li-mow ber-sar]*
grape	**anggur** *ahng-goor*
jackfruit	**buah nangka** *boo-ah nahng-kah*
kiwi fruit	**buah kiwi** *boo-ah ki-wi*
lemon	**lemon** *ley-mon*
lime	**limau nipis** *li-mow ni-pis*
mango	**mangga** *mahng-gah*
nutmeg	**buah pala** *boo-ah pah-lah*
orange	**oren** *o-reyn*
papaya	**betik** *ber-tik*
peach	**pic** *pich*
pear	**pear** *pear*
pineapple	**nanas** *nah-nahs*
plum	**buah plum** *boo-ah plum*
pomegranate	**buah delima** *boo-ah der-li-mah*
pomelo	**limau bali** *li-mow bah-li*
strawberry	**strawberi** *straw-bey-ri*
watermelon	**tembikai** *term-bi-k*

Dessert

Crushed ice with syrup, condensed milk and kidney beans	**ais kacang** *ah-is kah-chahng*	
Crushed ice with coconut milk, green jelly, red beans and brown sugar	**cendol** *cheyn-dol*	
Milk curd	**dadih** *dah-dih*	
Soy bean curd	**tauhu soya** *tow-hoo so-yah*	
Mixed fruit	**campuran buah-buahan** *chahm-poor-ahn boo-ah-boo-ah-hahn*	
Bean paste	**pes bijirin** *peys bi-ji-rin*	
Ice cream	**ais krim** *ah-is krim*	
Cake	**kek** *keyk*	
Peanut cake	**apom balik** *ah-pom bah-lik*	

Sauces & Condiments

Salt	**garam** *gah-rahm*
Pepper	**serbuk lada** *ser-book lah-dah*
Mustard	**biji sawi** *bi-ji sah-wi*

The best regional food is often served in hawker stalls, sold on the streets or in coffee shops. The main shopping malls will also have a range of food choices and an assortment of street foods can be found at **pasar malams** (night markets), which include restaurants, fast food places, food courts and places for nibbles. Although you can sometimes get authentic preparations in restaurants, the atmosphere at these venues cannot be replicated.

| Ketchup | **sos tomato** *sos to-mah-to* |
| Soy Sauce | **sos soya** *sos so-yah* |

At the Market

Where are the trolleys/ baskets?	**Di manakah troli/bakul?** *di mah-nah-kah tro-li/ bah-kool*
Where is…?	**Di manakah…?** *di mah-nah-kah …*
I'd like some of that/ this.	**Saya inginkan sedikit yang ini/itu.** *sah-yah ee-ngin-kahn ser-di-kit yahng ee-ni/ee-too*
Can I taste it?	**Bolehkah saya rasa?** *bo-ley-kah sah-yah rah-sah*
I'd like…	**Saya ingin…** *sah-yah ee-ngin …*
a kilo/half kilo of…	**sekilo/setengah kilo…** *ser-ki-lo/ser-tern-gah ki-lo*
a liter of…	**seliter…** *ser-li-ter …*

Measurements in Malaysia are metric and that applies to the weight of food too. If you tend to think in pounds and ounces, it's worth brushing up on what the metric equivalent is before you go shopping for fruit and veg in markets and supermarkets. Five hundred grams, or half a kilo, is a common quantity to order, and that converts to just over a pound (17.65 ounces, to be precise).

YOU MAY HEAR...

BOLEHKAH SAYA TOLONG ANDA?   Can I help you?
bo-ley-kah sah-yah to-long ahn-dah

APAKAH YANG ANDA MAHU?   What would you like?
ah-pah-kah yahng ahn-dah mah-hoo

ADA APA-APA LAGI?   Anything else?
ah-dah ah-pah-ah-pah lah-gi

ITU ... *ee-too...*   That's...

a piece of...	**sekeping...** *ser-ker-ping ...*
a slice of...	**sekerat...** *ser-ker-raht ...*
More/Less	**Lebih/Kurang** *ler-bih/koo-rahng*
How much?	**Berapakah harganya?** *ber-rah-pah-kah har-gah-nyah*
Where do I pay?	**Di manakah boleh saya bayar?** *di mah-nah-kah bo-ley sah-yah bah-yar*
A bag, please.	**Sila berikan beg.** *si-lah ber-ri-kahn beyg*
I'm being helped.	**Saya sedang dibantu.** *sah-yah ser-dahng di-bahn-too*

For Conversion Tables, see page 178.

YOU MAY SEE...

TARIKH LUPUS	best if used by...
KALORI	calories
BEBAS LEMAK	fat free
SIMPAN SEJUK	keep refrigerated
MUNGKIN MENGANDUNGI SISA-SISA	may contain traces of...
BOLEH GUNA KETUHAR GELOMBANG MIKRO	microwaveable
JUAL SEBELUM	sell by...
SESUAI UNTUK VEGETARIAN	suitable for vegetarians

In the Kitchen

bottle opener	**pembuka botol** *perm-boo-kah bo-tol*
bowl	**mangkuk** *mahng-kook*
can opener	**pembuka tin** *perm-boo-kah tin*
corkscrew	**skru pencungkil gabus** *skroo pern-choong-kil gah-boos*
cup	**cawan** *chah-wahn*
fork	**garpu** *gar-poo*
frying pan	**kuali** *koo-ah-li*
glass	**gelas** *ger-lahs*
(steak) knife	**pisau stik** *pi-sow (stik)*
measuring cup/spoon	**cawan/sudu penyukat** *cah-wahn/soo-doo peh-nyu-kat*
napkin	**napkin** *nap-kin*
plate	**pinggan** *ping-gahn*
pot	**periuk** *per-ri-ook*
spatula	**spatula** *spah-too-lah*
spoon	**sudu** *soo-doo*

While utensils are widely available, many locals will eat dishes such as **roti canai** and rice with their hands. If using your hands to eat, use your right hand, never your left, and scoop up the rice with your fingers and not your palm.

ESSENTIAL

The wine list/drink menu, please.	**Sila berikan senarai.** *si-lah ber-ri-kahn ser-nah-rai wain/mi-noom-mahn*
What do you recommend?	**Apakah yang anda cadangkan?** *ah-pah-kah yahng ahn-dah chah-dahng-kahn*
I'd like a bottle/glass of red/ white wine.	**Saya inginkan wain.** *sah-yah ee-ngin-kahn ser-bo-tol/ser-ger-lahs wain mey-rah/poo-tih*
The house wine, please.	**Sila berikan wain.** *si-lah ber-ri-kahn wain*
Another bottle/glass, please.	**Sila berikan.** *lagi si-lah ber-ri-kahn ser-bo-tol/ ser-ger-lahs lah-gi*
I'd like a local beer.	**Saya inginkan bir tempatan.** *sah-yah ee-ngin-kahn bir term-pah-tahn*
Can I buy you a drink?	**Bolehkah saya belanja anda minum?** *bo-ley-kah sah-yah ber-lahn-jah ahn-dah mi-noom*
Cheers!	**Minum!** *mi-noom*
A coffee/tea, please.	**Sila berikan** *si-lah ber-ri-kahn ko-pi/teyh*
Black.	**Hitam** *hee-tahm*
With...	**Dengan...** *der-ngahn*
milk	**susu** *soo-soo*
sugar	**gula** *goo-lah*
artificial sweetener	**pemanis tiruan** *per-mah-nis ti-roo-ahn*
A..., please.	**Sila berikan segelas.** *si-lah ber-ri-kahn ser-ger-lahs*
juice	**jus** *joos*
soda	**air soda** *ah-er so-dah*
(sparkling/still) water	**air (bergas/biasa)** *ah-er (ber-gahs/bee-ya-sah)*

Alcohol is expensive in Malaysia. A glass of wine may cost as much as a spirit. Alcohol is forbidden to Muslims, but it is available for purchase at pubs, hotels, restaurants and in Chinese eateries, as well as supermarkets in towns and tourist areas.

Non-alcoholic Drinks

coconut milk	**santan** *sahn-tahn*
coffee	**kopi** *ko-pi*
black	**hitam hi-tam**
with milk	**dengan susu** *der-ngahn soo-soo*
lemonade	**air limau** *ah-er li-mow*
(sparkling/still) water	**air** *ah-er (ber-gahs/bee-ya-sah)*
juice	**jus** *joos*
milk	**susu** *soo-soo*
soda	**soda** *so-dah*
(iced) tea	**(ais) teh** *(ah-is) tey*

Tap water is treated with fluoride and is safe for drinking. As a precaution, drink boiled water, especially in rural areas. Bottled water and mineral water can be purchased in major towns. Local coffee and tea pack a punch and may be too sweet for unsuspecting drinkers as they are sometimes served with condensed milk and sugar. Ipoh white coffee has won a wide following because of its creamy smooth taste and strong flavor. **Teh tarik** (pulled tea) is also a Malaysian favorite. Tea is poured back and forth with outstretched arms from a mug to a glass.

YOU MAY HEAR...

Bolehkah saya dapatkan anda minuman? Can I get you a drink?
bo-ley-kah sah-yah dah-paht-kahn
ahn-dah mi-noom-mahn

Dengan susu atau gula? With milk or sugar?
der-ngahn soo-soo ah-tow goo-lah

Air bergas? *ah-er ber-gas* Sparkling or still water?

Apéritifs, Cocktails & Liqueurs

brandy	**brandi** *brandy*
gin	**gin** *gin*
rum	**rum** *rum*
scotch	**scotch** *scotch*
tequila	**tequila** *teq-key-lah*
vodka	**vodka** *vod-kah*
whisky	**whisi** *wis-ki*

Beer

...beer	**bir...** *bir ...*
bottled/draft	**botol/draf/tin**
	bo-tol/drahf/tin
dark/light	**gelap/ringan**
	ger-lahp/ri-ngahn
lager/pilsener	**lager/pilsener** *lar-ger/pils-ner*
local/imported	**tempatan/diimport**
	term-pah-tahn/di-im-port
non-alcoholic	**tak beralkohol** *takh ber-al-koh-hol*

Wine

...wine	**wain** *wain*
red	**merah** *mey-rah*
white	**jernih** *jer-nih*
house/table	**rumah/meja** *roo-mah/mey-jah*
dry/sweet	**kering/manis** *ker-ring/mah-nis*
sparkling	**wain bergas [berkarbonat]** *wain ber-gahs [ber-kar-bo-naht]*
champagne	**champagne** *cham-payne*
dessert wine	**wain desert** *wain dee-sert*

Local brews include toddy and rice wines such as **tuak** and **li hing**. **Toddy** is made from the fermented sap of coconut palm. If sampling this brew, make sure it comes from a regulated source.

On the Menu

anchovy	**ikan bilis**	*ee-kahn bi-lis*
aperitif	**aperitif**	*ap-per-ee-tif*
apple	**epal**	*ey-pahl*
artichoke	**articok**	*ar-ti-chok*
artificial sweetener	**pemanis tiruan**	*per-mah-nis ti-roo-ahn*
asparagus	**pucuk asparagus**	*poo-cook ahs-pah-rah-goos*
avocado	**avocado**	*av-o-cah-doh*
banana	**pisang**	*pi-sahng*
bass	**ikan bes**	*ee-kahn beys*
bay leaf	**daun gulai**	*dah-oon goo-lai*
bean	**kacang**	*kah-chahng*
bean sprout	**taugeh**	*tow-gey*
beef	**daging lembu**	*dah-ging lerm-boo*
beer	**bir**	*bir*
brandy	**brandi**	*bran-dee*
bread	**roti**	*ro-ti*
breast (of chicken)	**dada (ayam)**	*dah-dah (ah-yahm)*
broth	**sup**	*soop*
butter	**mentega**	*mern-tey-gah*
cabbage	**kubis**	*koo-bis*
cake	**kek**	*keyk*
candy [sweets]	**gula-gula**	*goo-lah-goo-lah*
caramel	**caramel**	*kah-rah-meyl*
carrot	**lobak merah**	*lo-bahk mey-rah*
cashew	**gajus**	*gah-joos*
cauliflower	**kubis bunga**	*koo-bis boo-ngah*
celery	**daun sedari**	*dah-oon ser-dah-ri*
cereal	**bijian**	*bi-ji-ahn*
cheese	**keju**	*key-joo*

chestnut	**buah berangan**	*boo-ah ber-rah-ngahn*
chicken	**ayam**	*ah-yahm*
chickpea	**kacang kuda**	*kah-chahng koo-dah*
chili pepper[capsicum]	**lada benggala**	*lah-dah berng-gah-lah*
chives	**kucai**	*koo-chai*
chocolate	**coklat**	*cok-laht*
chopped meat	**potongan daging**	*po-to-ngahn dah-ging*
cider	**cider [jus epal awet]**	*[joos ey-pahl ah-weyt]*
cilantro [coriander]	**biji ketumbar**	*bi-ji ker-toom-bar*
cinnamon	**kulit kayu manis**	*koo-lit kah-yoo mah-nis*
clam	**kima (sejenis siput besar)**	*ki-mah (ser-jer-nis si-poot ber-sar)*
clove	**bunga cengkih**	*boo-ngah cherng-kih*
coconut	**kelapa**	*ker-lah-pah*
cod	**ikan kod**	*ee-kahn kod*
coffee	**kopi**	*ko-pi*
consommé	**sup jernih**	*soop jer-nih*
cookie [biscuit]	**biskut**	*bis-koot*
crab	**ketam**	*ker-tahm*
crabmeat	**daging ketam**	*dah-ging ker-tahm*
cracker	**kraker**	*krah-ker*
cream	**krim**	*krim*
cream, whipped	**krim putar**	*krim poo-tar*
cream cheese	**keju krim**	*key-joo krim*
cucumber	**timun**	*ti-moon*
cumin	**kumin**	*koo-min*
curry leaves	**daun kari**	*dah-oon kah-ri*
custard	**kastard**	*kahs-tahd*
dates	**kurma**	*koor-mah*
dessert wine	**wain desert**	*wain dee-sert*
duck	**itik**	*ee-tik*

dumpling	**ladu** *lah-doo*
eel	**ikan belut** *ee-kahn ber-loot*
egg	**telur** *ter-loor*
egg yolk/white	**telur kuning/putih** *ter-loor koo-ning/poo-tey*
eggplant [aubergine]	**terung ungu** *ter-roong oo-ngoo*
fennel	**jintan hitam** *jin-tahn hi-tahm*
fig	**pokok ara** *po-kok ah-rah*
fish	**ikan** *ee-kahn*
french fries	**kentang goreng** *kern-tahng go-reyng*
fritter (banana fritter)	**goreng bersadur (pisang goreng)** *go-reyng ber-sah-door (pi-sahng go-reyng)*
fruit	**buah-buahan** *boo-ah-boo-ah-ahn*
game	**daging binatang liar** *dah-ging bi-nah-tahng li-ah*
garlic	**bawang putih** *bah-wahng poo-tih*
gherkin	**timun gerkin** *ti-moon ger-kin*
giblet	**organ dalaman ayam** *or-gahn dah-lah-mahn ah-yahm*
gin	**gin** *gin*
ginger	**halia** *hah-lee-ya*
goat	**kambing** *kahm-bing*
goat cheese	**keju kambing** *key-joo kahm-bing*

goose	**angsa** *ahng-sah*
grapefruit	**limau gedang [limau besar]** *li-mow ger-dahng [li-mow ber-sar]*
grapes	**anggur** *ahng-goor*
green bean	**kacang hijau** *kah-chahng hee-jow*
guava	**jambu batu** *jahm-boo bah-too*
haddock	**hadok** *hah-dok*
halibut	**halibut** *hal-ee-but*
ham	**ham** *ham*
hamburger	**hamburger** *ham-bur-ger*
hazelnut	**kacang hazel** *kah-chahng hazel*
hen	**ayam betina** *ah-yahm ber-ti-nah*
herb	**herba** *her-bah*
herring	**ikan hering** *ee-kahn her-ring*
honey	**madu** *mah-doo*
hot dog	**roti dengan sosej** *ro-ti der-ngahn so-seyj*
hot pepper sauce	**sos lada pedas** *sos lah-dah per-dahs*
ice (cube)	**ais (ketulan)** *ah-is (ker-tool-lahn)*
ice cream	**ais krim** *ah-is krim*
jam	**jem** *jeym*
jelly	**agar-agar** *ah-gar-ah-gar*

juice	**jus** *joos*
ketchup	**sos tomato** *sos to-mah-to*
lamb	**anak kambing** *ah-nahk kahm-bing*
leek	**bawang kucai** *bah-wahng koo-chai*
lemon	**lemon** *ley-mon*
lemongrass	**serai** *ser-rai*
lemonade	**air limau (lemon)** *ah-er li-mow*
lentil	**lentil** *leyn-til*
lettuce	**selada** *ser-lah-dah*
lime	**limau nipis** *li-mow ni-pis*
liquor	**arak** *ah-rahk*
liver	**hati** *hah-ti*
lobster	**udang galah** *oo-dahng gah-lah*
longan fruit	**buah longan** *boo-ah lon-gahn*
mackerel	**sejenis ikan kembung** *ser-jer-nis ee-kahn kerm-boong*
mandarin orange	**limau mandarin** *li-mow mahn-dah-rin*
mango	**mangga** *mahng-gah*
margarine	**margarine** *mar-jar-een*
marmalade	**jem marmalade** *jeym marmalade*
mayonnaise	**mayones** *mah-yo-neys*

meat	**daging** *dah-ging*
milk	**susu** *soo-soo*
milk shake	**susu goncang** *soo-soo gon-chahng*
mint	**pudina** *poo-di-nah*
monkfish	**ikan biarawan** *ee-kahn bee-ya-rah-wahn*
mushroom	**cendawan** *chern-dah-wahn*
mussel	**siput sudu** *si-poot soo-doo*
mustard	**biji sawi** *bi-ji sah-wi*
mutton	**daging kambing** *dah-ging kahm-bing*
noodle	**mee** *mee*
nutmeg	**buah pala** *boo-ah pah-lah*
nuts	**kacang** *kah-chahng*
octopus	**sotong kurita** *so-tong koo-ri-tah*
okra [lady's finger]	**bendi** *beyn-di*
olive	**buah zaitun** *boo-ah zai-toon*
olive oil	**minyak buah zaitun** *min-yahk boo-ah zai-toon*
omelet	**telur dadar** *ter-loor dah-dar*
onion	**bawang merah** *bah-wahng mey-rah*
orange	**oren [limau]** *o-reyn [li-mow]*
oregano	**oregano** *or-ee-gah-noh*
organ meat [offal]	**daging organ dalaman** *dah-ging or-gahn dah-lah-mahn*
ox	**lembu jantan** *lerm-boo jahn-tahn*
oxtail	**ekor lembu** *ey-kor lerm-boo*
oyster	**tiram** *ti-rahm*
palm sugar	**gula Melaka** *goo-lah mer-lah-kah*
pancake	**penkek** *peyn-keyk*
papaya	**betik** *ber-tik*
paprika	**paprika** *pah-pree-kah*
pastry	**pastry** *pahs-tree*
peach	**pic** *pich*

peanut [groundnut]	**kacang tanah** *kah-chahng tah-nah*
pear	**pear** *pear*
peas	**kacang pis** *kah-chahng pis*
pecan	**kacang pecan** *kah-chahng per-kahn*
pepper (black/white)	**serbuk lada (hitam/putih)**
	ser-book lah-dah (hi-tahm/poo-tih)
pepper [chilli]	**lada** *lah-dah*
pheasant	**burung kuang** *boo-roong koo-ahng*
pickle	**acar** *ah-char*
pie	**pai** *pai*
pineapple	**nanas** *nah-nahs*
pizza	**pizza** *piz-zah*
plum	**buah plum** *boo-ah plum*
pomegranate	**buah delima** *boo-ah der-li-mah*
pork	**daging babi** *dah-ging bah-bi*
port	**sejenis wain** *ser-jer-nis wain*
potato	**ubi kentang** *oo-bi kern-tahng*
potato chips [crisps]	**keropok ubi kentang** *ker-ro-pok oo-bi kern-tahng*
poultry	**ayam dan itik** *ah-yahm dahn ee-tik*
prune	**buah prun** *boo-ah proon*
pumpkin	**labu** *lah-boo*

quail	**burung puyuh** *boo-roong poo-yooh*
rabbit	**arnab** *ah-nahb*
radish	**lobak putih** *lo-bahk poo-tih*
raisin	**kismis** *kis-mis*
red cabbage	**kubis merah** *koo-bis mey-rah*
relish	**pembuka selera** *perm-boo-kah ser-ler-rah*
rice	**nasi** *nah-si*
roast	**panggang** *pahng-gahng*
roast beef	**daging lembu panggang** *dah-ging lerm-boo pahng-gahng*
rum	**rum** *rum*
salad	**salad** *sal-ad*
salami	**salami** *sal-ah-mee*
salmon	**ikan salmon** *ee-kahn salmon*
salt	**garam** *gah-rahm*
sardine	**sardine** *sar-din*
sauce	**sos** *sos*
sausage	**sosej** *so-seyj*
scallion [spring onion]	**daun bawang** *dah-oon bah-wahng*
scallop	**kapis/kekapis** *kah-pis/ker-kah-pis*
scotch	**scotch** *scotch*

sea bass	**ikan bes laut**	*ee-kahn beys lah-oot*
sea perch	**ikan kerakap**	*ee-kahn ker-rah-kahp*
seafood	**makanan laut**	*mah-kahn-nahn lah-oot*
seaweed	**rumpai laut**	*room-pai lah-oot*
shallot	**bawang merah**	*bah-wahng mey-rah*
shank	**daging paha/betis**	*dah-ging pah-hah/ber-tis*
shellfish	**kerang-kerangan**	*ker-rahng ker-rah-ngahn*
sherry	**arak syeri**	*ah-rahk syey-ri*
shoulder	**daging bahagian bahu**	
	dah-ging bah-hah-gi-ahn bah-hoo	
shrimp	**udang**	*oo-dahng*
silver carp	**ikan kap perak**	*ee-kahn kahp pey-rahk*
sirloin	**daging batang pinang**	
	dah-ging bah-tahng pi-nahng	
snack	**snek**	*sneyk*
snail	**siput**	*si-poot*
soda	**soda**	*so-dah*
soup	**sup**	*soop*
sour cream	**krim masam**	*krim mah-sahm*
soy [soya]	**soya**	*so-yah*
soy sauce	**sos soya**	*sos so-yah*
soybean [soya bean]	**kacang soya**	*kah-chahng so-yah*
soymilk [soya milk]	**susu soya**	*soo-soo so-yah*
spaghetti	**spageti**	*spah-gey-ti*
spices	**rempah**	*rerm-pah*
spinach	**bayam**	*bah-yahm*
spirits	**arak**	*ah-rahk*
squash	**labu**	*lah-boo*
squid	**sotong**	*so-tong*
steak	**stik**	*stik*
strawberry	**strawberi**	*straw-bey-ri*

sugar	**gula** *goo-lah*
sweets	**gula-gula** *goo-lah-goo-lah*
sweet and sour sauce	**sos masam manis** *sos mah-sahm mah-nis*
sweet corn	**jagung manis** *jah-goong mah-nis*
sweet pepper	**lada manis** *lah-dah mah-nis*
sweet potato	**ubi kayu** *oo-bi kah-yoo*
sweetener	**pemanis** *per-mah-nis*
swordfish	**ikan todak** *ee-kahn to-dahk*
syrup	**sirap** *si-rahp*
tamarind	**asam jawa** *ah-sahm jah-wah*
tangerine	**limau tangerine** *li-mow tahn-ger-rin*
tea	**teh** *tey*
tofu	**tauhu** *tow-hoo*
toast	**roti bakar** *ro-ti bah-kar*
tomato	**tomato** *to-mah-to*
tongue	**lidah** *li-dah*
tonic water	**air tonik** *ah-er to-nik*
tripe	**perut haiwan/babat** *per-root hai-wahn/bah-baht*
trout	**ikan trout** *ee-kahn trout*
tuna	**ikan tuna** *ee-kahn tuna*
turkey	**ayam belanda** *ah-yahm ber-lahn-dah*

turnip	**lobak putih** *lo-bahk poo-tih*
vanilla	**vanilla** *van-ill-lah*
veal	**daging anak lembu** *dah-ging ah-nahk lerm-boo*
vegetable	**sayur-sayuran** *sah-yoor-sah-yoor-rahn*
venison	**daging rusa** *dah-ging roo-sah*
vinegar	**cuka** *choo-kah*
vodka	**vodka** *vod-kah*
waffle	**kek wafel** *keyk wah-ferl*
walnut	**kacang walnut** *kah-chahng walnut*
watercress	**selada air** *ser-lah-dah ah-er*
watermelon	**tembikai** *term-bi-kai*
wheat	**gandum** *gahn-doom*
whisky	**wiski** *wis-ki*
wine	**wain** *wain*
yogurt	**yogurt** *yoh-gurt*
zucchini [courgette]	**zukini** *zoo-ki-ni*

People

ESSENTIAL

Hello!	**Helo!** *hey-lo*
How are you?	**Apa khabar?** *ah-pah khah-bar*
Fine, thanks.	**Khabar baik.** *khah-bar ba-eek*
Excuse me!	**Maafkan saya!** *mah-ahf-kahn sah-yah*
Do you speak English?	**Adakah anda bercakap dalam Bahasa Inggeris?** **ah-dah-kah ahn-dah** *ber-chah-kahp dah-lahm Bah-hah-sah Ing-ger-ris*
What's your name?	**Apakah nama anda?** *ah-pah-kah nah-mah ahn-dah*
My name is...	**Nama saya ialah...** *nah-mah sah-yah ee-ya-lah*
Nice to know you.	**Gembira berkenalan dengan anda.** *germ-bi-rah ber-ker-nah-lahn der-ngahn ahn-dah*
Where are you from?	**Anda datang dari mana?** *ahn-dah dah-tahng dah-ri mah-nah*
I'm from the U.S./U.K.	**Saya datang dari U.S./U.K.** *sah-yah dah-tahng da-ri U.S./U.K.*
What do you do?	**Apakah pekerjaan anda?** *ah-pah-kah per-ker-jah-ahn ahn-dah*
I work as...	**Saya bekerja sebagai...** *sah-yah ber-ker-jah ser-bah-gai...*
I work for...	**Saya bekerja untuk...** *sah-yah ber-ker-jah oon-tuk...*
I'm a student.	**Saya seorang pelajar** *sah-yah ser-o-rahng per-lah-jar*
I'm retired.	**Saya seorang pesara** *sah-yah ser-o-rahng per-sah-rah*
Do you like...?	**Adakah anda suka...?** *ah-dah-kah ahn-dah soo-kah...*
Goodbye.	**Selamat tinggal.** *ser-lah-maht ting-gahl*

Encik *ern-chik*	Mr
Puan *poo-ahn*	Madam/Mrs
Cik *chik*	Miss/Ms

You may also come across titles like **Tun**, **Datuk Seri** or **Datuk** for men, **Datin** or **Puan Seri** for women, and **Yang Berhormat**. These are titles awarded to individuals who have made noteworthy contributions to society. They usually hold high positions in society, and can often be politicians.

Language Difficulties

Do you speak English?	**Adakah anda bercakap dalam Bahasa Inggeris?** *ah-dah-kah ahn-dah ber-chah-kahp dah-lahm Bah-hah-sah Ing-ger-ris*
Does anyone here speak English?	**Adakah sesiapa di sini yang boleh bercakap dalam Bahasa Inggeris?** *ah-dah-kah ser-siah-pah di si-ni yahng bo-ley ber-chah-kahp dah-lahm Bah-hah-sah Ing-ger-ris*
I don't speak Malay.	**Saya tidak boleh bercakap dalam Bahasa Melayu.** *sah-yah ti-dahk bo-ley ber-chah-kahp dah-lahm Bah-hah-sah Mer-lah-yoo*
Can you speak more slowly?	**Bolehkah anda bercakap dengan lebih perlahan?** *bo-ley-kah ahn-dah ber-chah-kahp der-ngahn ler-bih per-lah-han*
Can you repeat that?	**Bolehkah anda ulang semula?** *bo-ley-kah ahn-dah oo-lahng ser-moo-lah*
Excuse me?	**Maafkan saya?** *mah-ahf-kahn sah-yah*
Can you spell it?	**Apakah itu tadi?** *ah-pah-kah ee-too tah-di*
Please write it down.	**Sila tuliskannya.** *si-lah too-lis-kahn-nyah*

Can you translate this into English for me?	**Bolehkah anda menterjemahkannya ke dalam Bahasa Inggeris untuk saya?** *bo-ley-kah ahn-dah mern-ter-jer-mah-kahn-nyah ker dah-lahm Bah-hah-sah Ing-ger-ris oon-tuk sah-yah*
What does this/that mean?	**Apakah makna ini/itu?** *ah-pah-kah mahk-nah ee-ni/ ee-too*
I understand.	**Saya faham** *sah-yah fah-hahm*
I don't understand.	**Saya tidak faham** *sah-yah ti-dahk fah-hahm*
Do you understand?	**Adakah anda faham?** *ah-dah-kah ahn-dah fah-hahm*

YOU MAY HEAR...

Saya hanya boleh bercakap sedikit Bahasa Inggeris. *sah-yah hahn-yah bo-ley ber-chah-kahp ser-di-kit Bah-hah-sah Ing-ger-ris*	I only speak a little English.
Saya tidak boleh bercakap dalam Bahasa Inggeris. *sah-yah ti-dahk bo-ley ber-chah-kahp dah-lahm Bah-hah-sah Ing-ger-ris*	I don't speak English.

Making Friends

Hello!	**Helo!** *hey-lo*
Good afternoon.	**Selamat tengah hari** *ser-lah-maht ter-ngah hah-ri*
Good evening.	**Selamat petang.** *ser-lah-maht per-tahng*
My name is...	**Nama saya ialah...** *nah-mah sah-yah ee-ya-lah...*
What's your name?	**Apakah nama anda?** *ah-pah-kah nah-mah ahn-dah*

| I'd like to introduce you to... | **Saya ingin memperkenalkan anda kepada...** *sah-yah ee-ngin merm-per-ker-nahl-kahn ahn-dah ker-pah-dah ...* |
| How are you? | **Apa khabar?** *ah-pah khah-bar* |

I'd like to introduce you to...

Saya ingin memperkenalkan anda kepada... *sah-yah ee-ngin merm-per-ker-nahl-kahn ahn-dah ker-pah-dah ...*

Pleased to meet you.

Gembira berjumpa anda. *germ-bi-rah ber-joom-pah ahn-dah*

How are you?

Apa khabar? *ah-pah khah-bar*

Fine, thanks. And you?

Khabar baik, terima kasih. *khah-bar ba-ik, ter-ri-mah kah-sih*

In the Malay language, both **anda** and **kamu** refer to the pronoun 'you' and can be used interchangeably. However, **anda** is more polite whereas **kamu** is more casual. In a formal setting, **anda** is usually used. In this book, **anda** is used for consistency. Similarly, both **saya** and **aku** refer to the pronoun 'I', but **saya** is used throughout this book.

Travel Talk

I'm here...	**Saya ke sini...** *sah-yah ker si-ni*
on business	**untuk bisnes** *oon-tuk bis-neys*
on vacation [holiday]	**untuk bercuti** *oon-tuk ber-choo-ti*
studying	**untuk belajar** *oon-tuk ber-lah-jar*
I'm staying for...	**Saya akan tinggal untuk...** *sah-yah ah-kahn ting-gahl oon-tuk...*
I've been here...	**Saya sudah berada...di sini.** *sah-yah soo-dah ber-rah-dah...di si-ni*
a day	**sehari** *ser-har-ri*
a week	**seminggu** *ser-ming-goo*
a month	**sebulan** *ser-boo-lahn*
Where are you from?	**Anda datang dari mana?** *ahn-dah dah-tahng dah-ri mah-nah*
I'm from...	**Saya datang dari...** *sah-yah dah-tahng dah-ri...*

For Numbers, see page 173.

For Numbers, see page 173.

Personal

Who are you with?	**Anda datang dengan siapa?** *ahn-dah dah-tahng der-ngahn siah-pah*
I'm here alone.	**Saya datang sendiri.** *sah-yah dah-tahng sern-di-ri*
I'm with...	**Saya datang dengan...** *sah-yah dah-tahng der-ngahn...*
my husband/wife	**suami/isteri** *soo-ah-mi/is-ter-ri*
my boyfriend	**teman lekaki** *ter-mahn ler-lah-ki*
girlfriend	**teman wanita** *ter-mahn wah-ni-tah*
a friend	**kawan** *kah-wahn*
friends	**kawan-kawan** *kah-wahn-kah-wahn*
a colleague	**rakan sekerja** *rah-kahn ser-ker-jah*
When's your birthday?	**Bilakah hari jadi anda?** *bi-lah-kah hah-ri jahdi ahndah*

How old are you?	**Berapakah umur anda** *ber-rah-pah-kah oo-moor ahn-dah*
I'm...	**Saya...** *sah-yah...*
Are you married?	*ah-dah-kah ahn-dah ter-lah ber-kah-win*
I'm...	**Saya...** *sah-yah*
single/in a relationship	**masih bujang/sedang menjalin perhubungan** *mah-sih boo-jahng/ser-dahng mern-jah-lin per-hoo-boo-ngahn*
engaged	**sedang bertunang** *ser-dahng ber-too-nahng*
married	**telah berkahwin** *ter-lah ber-kah-win*
divorced	**telah bercerai** *ter-lah ber-cher-rai*
separated	**hidup berasingan** *hi-doop ber-rah-sing-ahn*
widowed	**balu** *bah-loo*
Do you have children/ grandchildren ?	**Adakah anda mempunyai anak/cucu-cicit?** *ah-dah-kah ahn-dah merm-poon-yah-i ah-nahk/ choo-choo-chi-chit*

For the Dictionary, see page 181.

Malaysians smile a lot, and are more often than not, polite, helpful, hospitable and friendly. However, it is wise to be on your guard and beware of possible scams and requests to meet 'a relative who has always wanted to visit your country'.

Work & School

| What do you do for a living? | **Apakah pekerjaan anda?** *ah-pah-kah per-ker-jah-ahn ahn-dah* |
| What are you studying? | **Apakah jurusan anda?** *ah-pah-kah joo-roo-sahn ahn-dah* |

I'm learning Malay.	**Saya sedang belajar Bahasa Melayu.** *sah-yah ser-dahng ber-lah-jar Bah-hah-sah Mer-lah-yoo*
I...	**Saya...** *sah-yah...*
work full-/	**sepenuh masa/sambilan** *ser-per-nooh mah-sah/*
part-time	*sam-bee-lahn*
am unemployed	**sedang menganggur** *ser-dahng merng-ahng-goor*
work at home	**bekerja di rumah** *ber-ker-jah di roo-mah*
Who do you work for?	**Anda bekerja untuk siapa?** *ahn-dah ber-ker-jah oon-tuk siah-pah*
I work for...	**Saya bekerja untuk...** *sah-yah ber-ker-jah oon-tuk*
Here's my business card.	**Ini kad perniagaan saya.** *ee-ni kahd per-nia-gah-ahn sah-yah*

For Business Travel, see page 145.

Weather

What's the forecast?	**Apakah ramalan cuaca?** *ah-pah-kah rah-mahl-ahn choo-ah-chah*
What beautiful/ terrible weather!	**Cuaca baik/Cuaca buruk!** *choo-ah-chah ba-ik/ choo-ah-chah boo-ruk*
It's...	**Cuaca hari ini...** *choo-ah-chah hah-ri ee-ni...*
cool/warm	**dingin/hangat** *di-ngin/hah-ngaht*

cold/hot	**sejuk/panas** *ser-jook/pah-nahs*
rainy/sunny	**hujan/cerah** *hoo-jahn/cher-rah*
snowy/icy	**bersalji/berais** *ber-sal-ji/ber-ah-is*
Do I need a jacket/ an umbrella ?	**Adakah saya perlu membawa sehelai jaket/ sekaki payung?** *ah-dah-kah sah-yah per-loo merm-bah-wah ser-hi-lai jah-keyt /ser-kah-ki pah-yoong*

For Temperature, see page 179.

Romance

ESSENTIAL

Would you like to go out for a drink/dinner ?	**Mahukah anda keluar untuk minum/makan malam?** *mah-hoo-kah ahn-dah ker-loo-ah oon-tuk mi-noom/ mah-kahn mah-lahm*
What are your plans for tonight/tomorrow?	**Apakah rancangan anda untuk malam ini/esok?** *ah-pah-kah rahn-chah-ngahn ahn-dah oon-tuk mah-lahm ee-ni/ey-sok*
Can I have your number?	**Bolehkah bagi saya nombor anda?** *bo-ley-kah bah-gi sah-yah nom-bor ahn-dah*
Can I join you?	**Bolehkah saya menemani anda?** *bo-ley-kah sah-yah mer-ner-mah-ni ahn-dah*
Can I get [treat] you a drink?	**Bolehkah saya belanja anda segelas minuman?** *bo-ley-kah sah-yah ber-lan-jah ahn-dah ser-ger-lahs mi-noom-mahn*
I like/love you.	**Saya suka/cinta pada kamu.** *sah-yah soo-kah/chin-tah pah-dah kah-moo*

The Dating Game

Would you like to go out…?	**Awak nak keluar…?** *Ah-wak nahk kel-oo-ar…*
for coffee	**minum kopi** *mi-noom ko-pi*
for a drink	**minum** *mi-noom*
to dinner	**makan malam** *mah-kahn mah-lahm*
What are your plans for…?	**Apakah rancangan anda untuk…?** *ah-pah-kah… rahn-chah-ngahn ahn-dah oon-tuk*
today	**hari ini** *hah-ri ee-ni*
tonight	**malam ini** *mah-lahm ee-ni*
tomorrow	**esok** *ey-sok*
this weekend	**hujung minggu ini** *hoo-joong ming-goo ee-ni*
Where would you like to go?	**Anda ingin pergi ke mana?** *ahn-dah ee-ngin per-gi ker mah-nah*
I'd like to go to…	**Saya ingin pergi ke…** *sah-yah ee-ngin per-gi ker…*
Do you like…?	**Adakah anda suka…?** *ah-dah-kah ahn-dah soo-kah*
Can I have your phone number/ e-mail ?	**Bolehkah bagi saya nombor telefon/alamat emel anda?** *bo-ley-kah bah-gi sah-yah nom-bor tey-ley-fon/ah-lah-maht ee-meyl ahn-dah*
Are you on Facebook/ Twitter?	**Awak ada Facebook/Twitter?** *Ah-wak ah-da Facebook/Twitter?*
Can I join you?	**Bolehkah saya menemani anda?** *bo-leh-kah sah-yah mer-ner-mah-ni ahn-dah*
You're very attractive.	**Anda sungguh menarik.** *ahn-dah soong-gooh mer-nah-reyk*
Let's go somewhere quieter.	**Mari kita pergi ke tempat yang lebih sunyi.** *mah-ri ki-tah per-gi keh term-paht yahng ler-bih soon-yi*

For Communications, see page 53.

While holding hands is common, displaying other forms of affection in public is considered bad form. The government is particular about upholding Islamic and Asian moral values, so such behaviour in public places is unacceptable, especially for locals or if you look like one.

Accepting & Rejecting

I'd love to.	**Saya berminat.** *sah-yah ber-mi-naht*
Where should we meet?	**Kita patut bertemu di mana?** *ki-tah pah-toot ber-ter-moo di mah-nah*
I'll meet you at the bar/your hotel.	**Saya akan menemui kamu di bar/hotel kamu.** *sah-yah ah-kahn mer-ner-moo-i kah-moo di bar/ ho-teyl kah-moo*
I'll come by at…	**Saya akan datang pada pukul…** *sah-yah ah-kahn dah-tahng pah-dah poo-kool…*
I'm busy.	**Saya sibuk.** *sah-yah si-book*
I'm not interested.	**Saya tidak berminat** *sah-yah ti-dahk ber-mi-naht*

| Leave me alone. | **Saya ingin bersendirian.** *sah-yah ee-ngin ber-sern-di-ri-ahn* |
| Stop bothering me! | **Jangan ganggu saya!** *jah-ngahn gahng-goo sah-yah* |

For Time, see page 175.

Getting Intimate

Can I hug/kiss you?	**Bolehkah saya memeluk/mencium kamu?** *bo-ley-kah sah-yah mer-mer-look/mern-chi-oom kah-moo*
Yes.	**Ya** *yah*
No.	**Tidak** *ti-dahk*
Stop!	**Berhenti!** *ber-hern-ti*
I love you.	**Saya cinta pada kamu.** *sah-yah chin-tah pah-dah kah-moo*

Sexual Preferences

Are you gay?	**Awak gay ke?** *Ah-wak gay ker*
I'm...	**Saya....** *sah-yah...*
heterosexual	**heteroseksual** *het-ero-seksual*
homosexual	**homoseksual** *ho-mo-seksual*
bisexual	**dwiseksual** *dwee-seksual*
Do you like men/ women?	**Awak suka lelaki/perempuan?** *Ah-wak suh-kah ler-lah-ki/pe-rehm-pu-ahn*

Be warned, Malaysians are generally reserved and may not be comfortable when asked forward questions regarding romance or sexuality.

Leisure Time

ESSENTIAL

Where's the tourist information office?	**Di manakah pejabat maklumat pelancong?** *di mah-nah-kah per-jah-baht mahk-loo-maht per-lahn-chong*
What are the main attractions (here)?	**Apakah tarikan-tarikan utama (di sini)?** *ah-pah-kah tah-rik-kahn-tah-rik-kahn oo-tah-mah (di si-ni)*
Are there tours in English?	**Adakah lawatan dalam Bahasa Inggeris?** *ah-dah-kah lah-wah-tahn dah-lahm Bah-hah-sah Ing-ger-ris*
Can I have a map	**Bolehkah bagi saya peta?** *bo-ley-kah bah-gi sah-yah per-tah*
Can I have a guide book?	**Bolehkah bagi saya buku panduan?** *bo-ley-kah bah-gi sah-yah boo-koo pahn-doo-ahn*

Tourist Information

Do you have information on...?	**Adakah anda mempunyai maklumat tentang...?** *ah-dah-kah ahn-dah merm-poon-yai mahk-loo-maht tern-tahng...*
Can you recommend...?	**Bolehkah anda mencadangkan...?** *bo-ley-kah ahn-dah mern-chah-dahng-kahn...*
a bus tour	**satu lawatan bas** *sah-too lah-wah-tahn bahs*
an excursion to...	**satu rombongan ke...** *sah-too rom-bo-ngahn ker...*
a tour of...	**rombongan...** *rohm-bo-ngahn...*

Tourism Malaysia (**www.tourism.gov.my**) has offices in every state. The offices vary in the amount of literature available, but there are usually comprehensive brochures on each state and sometimes local places of interest, and the officers are informed and helpful. The regional offices can also be contacted for information on reliable tour and travel operators, who have to be registered with them. In addition, both Sarawak and Sabah have their own state-run tourism offices.

On Tour

I'd like to go on the excursion to…	**Saya ingin pergi melancong ke…** *sah-yah ee-ngin per-gi mer-lahn-chong ker…*
When's the next tour?	**Bilakah lawatan yang berikutnya?** *bi-lah-kah lah-wah-tahn yajng ber-ri-koot-nyah*
Are there tours in English?	**Adakah lawatan dalam Bahasa Inggeris?** *ah-dah-kah lah-wah-tahn dah-lahm Bah-hah-sah Ing-ger-ris*
Is there an English guide book/audio guide?	**Ada buku panduan/audio panduan bahasa Inggeris?** *Ah-dah pahn-doo-ahn/au-di-o pahn-doo-ahn bah-hah-sah Ing-ger-ris?*
What time do we leave/return?	**Pukul berapakah kami akan berlepas/pulang?** *poo-kool ber-rah-pah-kah kah-mi ah-kahn ber-ler-pahs/ poo-lahng*
We'd like to see…	**Kami ingin melihat…** *kah-mi ee-ngin mer-li-haht…*
Can we stop here…?	**Bolehkah kami berhenti di sini…?** *boy-leh-kah kah-mi ber-hern-ti di si-ni…*
to take photos	**untuk mengambil gambar** *oon-tuk merng-ahm-bil gahm-bar*

for souvenirs	**untuk membeli cenderahati** *oon-tuk merm-ber-li chern-der-rah-hah-ti*
for the toilets	**untuk menggunakan bilik air** *oon-tuk merng-goo-nah-kahn bi-lik ah-er*
Is it disabled-accessible?	**Adakah ia mesra orang kurang upaya?** *ah-dah-kah ee-ya mers-rah o-rahng koo-rahng oo-pah-yah*

For Tickets, see page 19.

Seeing the Sights

Where's...?	**Di manakah...** *di mah-nah-kah...*
the battleground	**medan pertempuran** *meh-dahn per-tehm-poo-rahn*
the botanical garden	**taman botani** *tah-mahn bo-tah-ni*
the castle	**istana** *is-tah-nah*
the downtown	**pusat bandar** *poo-saht bahn-dar*
the fountain	**air pancutan** *ah-er pahn-choo-tahn*
the library	**perpustakaan** *per-poos-tah-kah-ahn*
the market	**pasar** *pah-sar*
the museum	**muzium** *moo-zi-oom*
the old town	**bandar lama** *bahn-dar lah-mah*
the opera house	**rumah opera** *roo-mah o-per-rah*

the palace	**istana** *is-tah-nah*
the park	**taman** *tah-mahn*
the rainforest	**hutan hujan** *hoo-tahn hoo-jahn*
the ruins	**runtuhan** *roon-too-hahn*
the shopping area	**tempat membeli-belah**
	term-paht merm-ber-li-ber-lah
the town square	**pusat pekan** *poo-saht per-kahn*
the wildlife center	**pusat hidupan liar** *poo-sat hee-do-pahn lee-ar*
Can you show me on the map?	**Bolehkah anda tunjukkan di atas peta?**
	boy-leh-kah ahn-dah toon-juk-kahn di ah-tahs per-tah
It's...	**Ia...** *ee-ya...*
amazing	**mengagumkan** *mer-ngah-goom-kahn*
beautiful	**cantik** *chahn-tik*
boring	**membosankan** *merm-bo-sahn-kahn*
interesting	**menarik** *mer-nah-rik*

Whenever you enter religious grounds, you must remove your shoes and socks. Proper clothing should also be worn at a temple: especially no short skirts for women and no skimpy shorts.

magnificent	**indah dan mengagumkan**
	in-dah dahn mer-ngah-goom-kahn
romantic	**romantik** *ro-mahn-tik*
strange	**pelik** *per-lik*
terrible	**teruk** *ter-rook*
ugly	**hodoh** *ho-doh*
I (don't) like it.	**Saya (tidak) suka.** *sah-yah (ti-dahk) soo-kah*

For Asking Directions, see page 37.

Religious Sites

Where's…?	**Di manakah…?** *Di-mah-nah-kah…*
the Catholic/	**gereja Katolik/Protestan** *ger-rey-jah Kah-to-lik/*
Protestant church	*Pro-teys-tahn*
the mosque	**masjid** *mahs-jid*
the shrine	**tugu ibadat** *too-goo ee-bah-daht*
	keramat [for Malay shrines] *ker-rah-maht*
the synagogue	**rumah ibadat orang Yahudi**
	roo-mah ee-bah-daht o-rahng Yah-hoo-di
the temple	**tokong [for Buddhist temples]** *to-kong*
	kuil [for Hindu temples] *koo-ill*
What time is the	**servis pada pukul berapa?** *ser-vis pah-dah poo-kool*
service?	*ber-rah-pah*

Shopping

ESSENTIAL

Where's the market?	**Di manakah pasar?** *di mah-nah-kah pah-sar*
Where is the mall [shopping centre]?	**Di manakah pasar raya [pusat membeli-belah]?** *di mah-nah-kah pah-sar rah-yah [poo-saht merm-ber-li-ber-lah]*
I'm just looking.	**Saya tengok-tengok sahaja.** *sah-yah tey-ngok-tey-ngok sah-hah-jah*
Can you help me?	**Bolehkah anda membantu saya?** *bo-ley-kah ahn-dah merm-bahn-too sah-yah*
I'm being helped.	**Saya sedang dibantu.** *sah-yah ser-dahng di-bahn-too*
How much?	**Berapakah harganya?** *ber-rah-pah-kah har-gah-nyah*
That one, please.	**Sila berikan yang itu.** *si-lah ber-ri-kahn yahng ee-too*
That's all.	**Itu sahaja.** *ee-too sah-hah-jah*
Where can I pay?	**Di manakah boleh saya bayar?** *di mah-nah-kah bo-ley sah-yah bah-yar*
I'll pay in cash	**Saya akan bayar dengan wang tunai.** *sah-yah ah-kahn bah-yar der-ngahn wahng too-nai*
I'll pay by credit card.	**Saya akan bayar dengan kad kredit.** *sah-yah ah-kahn bah-yar der-ngahn kahd krey-dit*
A receipt, please.	**Sila berikan resit.** *si-lah ber-ri-kahn rey-sit*

Malaysia is somewhat of a shopping haven. There are over 50 malls in Kuala Lumpur, and another 40 in neighboring Petaling Jaya. If the sheer number of malls isn't enough to ignite the shopping impulse, there's always the annual Malaysia Mega Sale carnival, usually held around the end of June/beginning of July up until early September. Expect heavy discounts, promotions and competitions to satisfy even the most seasoned shoppers.

At the Shops

Where's…?	**Di manakah…?**	*Di-mah-nah-kah…*
the antiques store	**kedai antik**	*ker-dai ahn-tik*
the bakery	**kedai roti**	*ker-dai ro-ti*
the bank	**bank**	*bahnk*
the bookstore	**kedai buku**	*ker-dai boo-koo*
the clothing store	**kedai pakaian**	*ker-dai pah-kai-ahn*
the delicatessen	**delikatesen**	*deli-kah-tess-an*
the department	**pusat membeli-belah**	*poo-saht merm-ber-li-ber-lah*
the gift shop	**kedai hadiah**	*ker-dai hah-diah*

the health food store	**kedai makanan sihat** *ker-dai mah-kah-nahn si-haht*
the jeweler	**kedai emas** *ker-dai er-mas*
the liquor store [off-licence]	**kedai arak (untuk diminum di tempat lain)** *ker-dai ah-rahk (oon-tuk di-mi-noom di term-paht lah-een)*
the market	**pasar** *pah-sar*
the music store	**kedai muzik** *ker-dai moo-zik*
the pastry shop	**kedai pastry** *ker-dai pahs-tri*
the pharmacy	**farmasi** *far-mah-si*
the produce [grocery] store	**kedai runcit** *ker-dai roon-chit*
the shoe store	**kedai kasut** *ker-dai kah-soot*
the shopping mall	**pusat membeli-belah** *poo-saht merm-ber-li-ber-lah*
the souvenir store	**kedai cenderahati** *ker-dai chern-der-rah-hah-ti*
the supermarket	**pasar raya** *pah-sar rah-yah*
the tobacconist	**penjual barang-barang tembakau.** *Pen-joo-al bah rahng- bah-rahng tehm-ba-kow*
the toy store	**kedai mainan** *ker-dai mah-een-nahn*

Ask an Assistant

When do you open/ close?	**Bilakah anda buka/tutup?** *bi-lah-kah ahn-dah boo-kah/too-tup*
the cashier	**juruwang** *joo-roo-wahng*
the escalator	**tangga gerak** *tahng-gah ger-rahk*
the elevator [lift]	**lif** *lif*
the fitting room	**bilik mencuba pakaian** *bi-lik mern-choo-bah pah-kai-ahn*
the store directory	**papan panduan kedai** *pah-pahn pahn-doo-ahn ker-dai*
Can you help me?	**Bolehkah anda membantu saya?** *bo-ley-kah ahn-dah merm-bahn-too sah-yah*

I'm just looking.	**Saya tengok-tengok sahaja.** *sah-yah tey-ngok-tey-ngok sah-hah-jah*
I'm being helped.	**Saya sedang dibantu.** *sah-yah ser-dahng di-bahn-too*
Do you have…?	**Adakah anda mempunyai…?** *ah-dah-kah ahn-dah merm-poo-nyai…*
Can you show me…?	**Bolehkah anda tunjukkan kepada saya…?** *bo-ley-kah ahn-dah toon-juk-kahn ker-pah-dah sah-yah…*
Can you ship it/ wrap it?	**Bolehkah anda hantarkannya/ bungkuskannya?** *bo-ley-kah ahn-dah hahn-tar-kahn-nyah/ boong-koos-kahn-nyah*
How much?	**Berapakah harganya?** *ber-rah-pah-kah har-gah-nyah*
That's all.	**Itu sahaja.** *ee-too sah-hah-jah*

For Souvenirs, see page 132.

YOU MAY HEAR…

Bolehkah saya menolong anda? *bo-ley-kah sah-yah mer-no-long ahn-dah*	Can I help you?
Sekejap [Nanti]. *ser-ker-jahp [nahn-ti]*	One moment. [Hold on.]
Apakah yang anda mahu? *ah-pah-kah yahng ahn-dah mah-hoo*	What would you like?
Ada apa-apa lagi? *ah-dah ah-pah-ah-pah lah-gi*	Anything else?

YOU MAY SEE...

ABUKA/TUTUP	open/closed
TUTUP UNTUK WAKTU MAKAN TENGAH HARI	closed for lunch
BILIK MENCUBA PAKAIAN	fitting room
JURUWANG	cashier
WANG TUNAI SAHAJA	cash only
KAD KREDIT DITERIMA	credit cards accepted
WAKTU PERNIAGAAN	business hours
KELUAR	exit

Personal Preferences

I'd like something...	**Saya inginkan sesuatu benda yang...** *sah-yah ee-ngin-kahn ser-soo-ah-too bern-dah yahng . . .*
cheap/expensive	**murah/mahal** *moo-rah/mah-hahl*
larger/smaller	**lebih besar/lebih kecil** *ler-bih ber-sar/ler-bih ker-chil*
from this region	**dari wilayah ini** *dah-ri wee-lah-yah ee-ni*
Around...Ringgit.	**Lebih kurang....Ringgit** *Ler-bih koo-rahng ....Ring-git*
Is it real?	**Adakah ia asli?** *ah-dah-kah ee-ya ahs-li*
Can you show me this/that?	**Bolehkah anda tunjukkan yang ini/itu?** *bo-ley-kah ahn-dah toon-juk-kahn yahng ee-ni/ee-too*
That's not quite what I want.	**Itu bukan benda yang saya mahu.** *ee-too boo-kahn bern-dah yahng sah-yah mah-hoo*
No, I don't like it.	**Tidak, saya tidak menyukainya.** *ti-dahk, sah-yah ti-dahk mer-nyoo-kai-nyah*
It's too expensive.	**Itu terlalu mahal.** *ee-too ter-lah-loo mah-hahl*
I have to think about it.	**Saya perlu mempertimbangkannya dahulu.** *sah-yah per-loo merm-per-tim-bahng-kahn-nyah dah-hoo-loo*

I'll take it.	**Saya akan membelinya.** *sah-yah ah-kahn merm-ber-li-nyah*

Paying & Bargaining

How much?	**Berapakah harganya?** *ber-rah-pah-kah har-gah-nyah*
I'll pay…	**Saya akan membayar…** *sah-yah ah-kahn merm-bah-yar . . .*

YOU MAY HEAR...

Bagaimanakah anda akan membayar? *bah-gai-mah-nah-kah ahn-dah ah-kahn merm-bah-yar*	How are you paying?
Kad kredit anda telah ditolak. *kahd krey-dit ahn-dah ter-lah di-to-lahk*	Your credit card has been declined.
Sila tunjukkan ID. *si-lah toon-juk-kahn ID*	ID, please.
Kami tidak menerima kad kredit. *kah-mi ti-dahk mer-ner-ri-mah kahd krey-dit*	We don't accept credit cards.
Kami hanya menerima wang tunai sahaja. *kah-mi hah-nyah mer-ner-ri-mah wahng too-nai sah-hah-jah*	Cash only, please.

in cash	**dengan wang tunai** *der-ngahn wahng too-nai*
by credit card	**dengan kad kredit** *der-ngahn kahd krey-dit*
by traveller's cheque	**dengan cek kembara** *der-ngahn cheyk kerm-bah-rah*
A receipt, please.	**Sila berikan resit.** *si-lah ber-ri-kahn rey-sit*
That's too much.	**Itu terlalu mahal.** *ee-too ter-lah-loo mah-hahl*
I'll give you…	**Saya akan memberi anda …** *sah-yah ah-kahn merm-ber-ri ahn-dah …*
I have only…Ringgit.	**Saya hanya ada….Ringgit.** *Sah-yah hah-nyar ah-dah…Ring-git*
Is that your best price?	**Adakah itu harga yang terbaik?** *ah-dah-kah ee-too har-gah yahng ter-baik*
Can you give me a discount?	**Bolehkah anda berikan saya diskaun?** *bo-ley-kah ahn-dah ber-ri-kahn sah-yah dis-kown*

For Numbers, see page 173.

Making a Complaint

I'd like…	**Saya ingin…** *sah-yah ee-ngin…*
to exchange this	**menukar benda ini** *mer-noo-kar bern-dah ee-ni*
a refund	**meminta bayaran balik** *mer-min-tah bah-yar-rahn bah-lik*
to see the manager	**berjumpa dengan pengurus** *ber-joom-pah der-ngahn pern-goo-roos*

Services

Can you recommend…?	**Bolehkah anda mencadangkan…?** *bo-ley-kah ahn-dah mern-chah-dahng-kahn…*
a barber	**seorang tukang gunting rambut** *ser-o-rahng too-kahng goon-ting rahm-boot*
a dry cleaner	**sebuah kedai dobi** *ser-boo-ah ker-dai do-bi*
a hairstylist	**seorang pendandan rambut** *ser-o-rahng pern-dahn-dahn rahm-boot*

a Laundromat [launderette]	**sebuah kedai dobi layan diri** *ser-boo-ah ker-dai do-bi lah-yahn di-ri*
a nail salon	**sebuah salun kuku** *ser-boo-ah sah-loon koo-koo*
a spa	**sebuah spa** *ser-boo-ah spah*
a travel agency	**sebuah agensi perlancongan** *ser-boo-ah ah-gern-si per-lahn-chong-ahn*
Can you…this?	**Bolehkah anda … ini?** *bo-ley-kah ahn-dah … ee-ni*
alter	**meminda** *mer-min-dah*
clean	**mencuci** *mern-choo-chi*
fix	**memperbaiki** *merm-per-bai-ki*
press	**menyeterika** *mern-yer-ter-ri-kah*
When will it be ready?	**Bilakah ia akan siap?** *bi-lah-kah ee-ya ah-kahn see-yap*

Hair & Beauty

I'd like…	**Saya ingin…** *sah-yah ee-ngin…*
an appointment for today/tomorrow	**membuat janji temu untuk hari ini/esok.** *merm-boo-aht jahn-ji ter-moo oon-tuk hah-ri ee-ni/ey-sok*
some color/ highlights	**sedikit warna/penyerlah** *ser-di-kit wahr-nah/ pern-yer-lah*

my hair styled/ blow-dried	**rambut saya digayakan /ditiup kering.** *rahm-boot sah-yah di-gah-yah-kahn/ di-ti-oop ker-ring*
a haircut	**menggunting rambut** *merng-goon-ting rahm-boot*
an eyebrow/ bikini wax	**Lilin alis/bikini** *Lee-lin ah-lees/bi-ki-ni*
a facial	**rawatan muka** *rah-wah-tahn moo-kah*
a manicure/ pedicure	**manikur/pedikur** *mah-ni-kur/peh-di-kur*
a (sports) massage	**urut (sukan)** *oo-rut (soo-kahn)*
A trim, please.	**Rapikan, ya.** *Rah-pee-kahn, yer.*
Not too short.	**Jangan terlalu pendek.** *jah-ngahn ter-lah-loo peyn-deyk*
Shorter here.	**Pendek lagi di sini.** *peyn-deyk lah-gi di sini*
Do you offer…?	**Awak menawarkan….?** *Ah-wak meh-nah-war-kahn…*
acupuncture	**akupunktur** *ah-koo-poonk-tur*
aromatherapy	**aromaterapi** *ah-ro-mah-ter-rah-pi*
oxygen	**Oksigen** *ox-ey-jen*
a sauna	**mandi sauna** *mahn-di sow-nah*

Antiques

How old is it?	**Berapakah umurnya?** *ber-rah-pah-kah oo-moor-nyah*
Do you have anything from the…period?	**Adakah anda mempunyai antic…daripada zaman…?** *ah-dah-kah ahn-dah merm-poon-yai ahn-tik…dah-ri-pah-dah zah-mahn*
Do I have to fill out any forms?	**Adakah saya perlu mengisi borang?** *ah-dah-kah sah-yah per-loo mer-ngi-si bo-rahng*
Is there a certificate of authenticity?	**Adakah ia mempunyai sijil keaslian?** *ah-dah-kah ee-ya merm-poon-yai si-jil ker-ahs-lee-yan*
Can you ship/wrap it?	**Bolehkah anda hantarkannya/ bungkuskannya?** *bo-ley-kah ahn-dah hahn-tar-kahn-nyah/ boong-koos-kahn-nyah*

Clothing

I'd like…	**Saya ingin…** *sah-yah ee-ngin…*
Can I try this on?	**Bolehkah saya mencuba pakaian ini?** *bo-ley-kah sah-yah mern-choo-bah pah-kai-ahn ee-ni*
It doesn't fit.	**Ia tidak sesuai.** *ee-ya ti-dahk ser-soo-ai*
It's too…	**Ia terlalu…** *ee-ya ter-lah-loo…*
big/small	**besar/kecil** *ber-sar/ker-chil*
short/long	**pendek/panjang** *peyn-deyk/pahn-jahng*
tight/loose	**ketat/longgar** *ker-taht/ ong-gar*

YOU MAY HEAR…

Nampak cantik pada anda. *nahm-pahk chahn-tik ah-pah ahn-dah*	That looks great on you.
Bolehkah ia muat? *bo-ley-kah ee-ya moo-aht*	How does it fit?
Kami tidak mempunyai saiz anda. *kah-mi ti-dahk merm-poon-yai sah-iz ahn-dah*	We don't have your size.

Jeans and T-shirts aside, fashion in Malaysia is varied and colorful. The Malay **baju kurung** and Indian **kurtha** are worn daily to work by women across ethnic line. Indian women wear **saris** and Muslim women wear the **tudung**. Muslim and Hindi men wear traditional outfits when they go for prayers. The Chinese population tend to only wear traditional wear during festive periods and for weddings. For the wealthier middle classes, designer brands are important.

Do you have this in size…?	**Adakah anda mempunyai saiz untuk yang ini?** *ah-dah-kah ahn-dah merm-poon-yai sah-iz oon-tuk yahng ee-ni*
Do you have this in a bigger/smaller size?	**Adakah anda mempunyai saiz yang lebih besar/ lebih kecil?** *ah-dah-kah ahn-dah merm-poon-yai sah-iz yahng ler-bih ber-sar/ler-bih ker-chil*

For Numbers, see page 173.

YOU MAY SEE…

LELAKI	men's
WANITA	women's
KANAK-KANAK	children's

Colors

I'd like something…	**Saya inginkan sesuatu yang berwarna…** *sah-yah ee-ngin-kahn ser-soo-ah-too yahng ber-war-nah*
beige	**kuning air** *koo-ning ah-er*
black	**hitam** *hi-tahm*

blue	**biru** *bi-roo*
brown	**perang** *pey-rahng*
green	**hijau** *hee-jow*
gray	**kelabu** *ker-lah-boo*
orange	**oren** *o-reyn*
pink	**merah jambu** *mey-rah jahm-boo*
purple	**ungu** *oo-ngoo*
red	**merah** *mey-rah*
white	**putih** *poo-tih*
yellow	**kuning** *koo-ning*

Clothes & Accessories

a backpack	**beg galas** *beyg gah-lahs*
a belt	**tali pinggang** *tah-li ping-gahng*
a bikini	**bikini** *bi-ki-ni*
a blouse	**blaus** *blah-oos*
a bra	**coli** *cho-li*
briefs [underpants]/ panties	**seluar dalam** *ser-loo-ah dah-lahm*
a coat	**kot** *kot*
a dress	**gaun** *ga-oon*
a hat	**topi** *to-pi*

a jacket	**jaket** *jah-keyt*
jeans	**jean** *jeen*
pajamas	**baju tidur** *bah-joo ti-doo*
pants [trousers]	**seluar panjang** *ser-loo-ah pahn-jahng*
pantyhose [tights]	**sarung kaki wanita** *sah-roong kah-ki wah-ni-tah*
a purse [handbag]	**beg duit wanita [beg tangan wanita]** *beyg doo-it wah-ni-tah [beyg tah-ngahn wah-ni-tah]*
a raincoat	**baju hujan** *bah-joo hoo-jahn*
a scarf	**scarf** *skahrf*
a shirt	**kemeja** *ker-may-ja*
shorts	**seluar pendek** *ser-loo-ah peyn-deyk*
a skirt	**skirt** *skirt*
socks	**sarung kaki** *sah-roong kah-ki*
a suit	**sut** *soot*
sunglasses	**cermin mata hitam** *cher-min mah-tah hi-tahm*
a sweater	**baju panas** *bah-joo pah-nahs*
a sweatshirt	**baju panas** *bah-joo pah-nahs*
a swimsuit	**baju renang** *bah-joo rer-nahng*
a T-shirt	**baju kemeja T** *bah-joo ker-mey-jah T*
a tie	**tali leher** *tah-li ley-her*
underwear	**baju dalam** *bah-joo dah-lahm*

Fabric

I'd like...	**Saya inginkan...** *sah-yah ee-ngin-kahn...*
cotton	**kain kapas** *ka-een kah-pahs*
denim	**kain denim** *ka-een dey-nim*
lace	**renda** *rern-dah*
leather	**kulit** *koo-lit*
linen	**kain linen** *ka-een li-nern*
silk	**kain sutera** *ka-een soo-ter-rah*
wool	**bulu biri-biri** *boo-loo bi-ri-bi-ri*
Is it machine washable?	**Bolehkah ia dicuci menggunakan mesin pembasuh?** *bo-ley-kah ee-ya di-choo-chi merng-goo-nah-kahn mer-sin perm-bah-sooh*

Batik cloth is often used to symbolise Malaysia. The national airline uses it for its uniforms. Batik shirts are recognised as men's formal attire and are compulsory dress at the nation's casino. Batik is also worn as sarongs and used for the traditional women's dress known as **baju kurung**. Silk brocades, known as **kain songket**, have always been the favored textiles of Malaysian royalty. Today, this elegant woven cloth is still the preferred wear at official events, not only for courtly occasions, but also for government functions. This material is most often used as traditional bridal wear, when both the bride and groom are dressed in sumptuous brocade outfits.

Shoes

I'd like...	**Saya inginkan...** *sah-yah ee-ngin-kahn...*
high-heels/flats	**kasut bertumit tinggi/tidak bertumit** *kah-soot ber-too-mit ting-gi/ti-dahk ber-too-mit*
	kasut lepak *kah-soot ler-pahk*

boots	**but** *boot*
loafers	**kasut lepak** *kah-soot ler-pahk*
sandals	**sandal** *sahn-dahl*
shoes	**kasut** *kah-soot*
slippers	**selipar** *ser-li-pah*
sneakers	**kasut sukan** *kah-soot soo-kahn*
Size...	**Dalam saiz...** *dah-lahm sah-iz...*

For Numbers, see page 173.

Sizes

small (S)	**kecil** *ker-chil*
medium (M)	**sederhana** *ser-der-hah-nah*
large (L)	**besar** *ber-sar*
extra large (XL)	**lebih besar** *ler-bih ber-sar*
petite	**kecil molek** *ker-chil mor-lek*
plus size	**saiz tambah** *sah-iz tahm-bah*

Newsagent & Tobacconist

| Do you sell English-language newspapers? | **Adakah anda menjual surat khabar Bahasa Inggeris?** *ah-dah-kah ahn-dah mern-joo-ahl soo-raht kha-bar Bah-hah-sah Ing-ger-ris* |
| I'd like... | **Saya inginkan...** *sah-yah ee-ngin-kahn...* |

candy [sweets]	**gula-gula** *goo-lah-goo-lah*	
chewing gum	**gula-gula getah** *goo-lah-goo-lah ger-tah*	
a chocolate bar	**bar coklat** *bar chok-lat*	
a cigar	**sebatang cerut** *ser-bah-tahng cher-root*	
a pack/carton of cigarettes	**sekotak rokok** *ser-ko-tahk ro-kok*	
a lighter	**pemetik api** *per-mer-tik ah-pi*	
a magazine	**senaskah majalah** *ser-boo-ah mah-jah-lah*	
matches	**sekotak mancis** *ser-ko-tahk mahn-chis*	
a newspaper	**senaskah surat khabar** *soo-raht kha-bar*	
a pen	**pen** *pen*	
a postcard	**sekeping poskad** *ser-ker-ping pos-kahd*	
a road/town map of...	**sebuah peta jalan/Bandar...** *ser-boo-ah per-tah jah-lan/Bahn-dar...*	
stamps	**setem** *ser-teym*	

In Malaysia, there are newspapers and magazines, as well as TV stations featuring programs in Malay, English, Indonesian, Chinese and Tamil. Most newspapers also have online editions.

Photography

I'd like...camera.	**Saya inginkan sebuah kamera...** *sah-yah ee-ngin-kahn ser-boo-ah kah-mer-ra...*	
an automatic	**automatik** *ow-to-mah-tik*	
a digital	**digital** *di-gi-tahl*	
a disposable	**pakai buang** *pah-kai boo-ahng*	
I'd like...	**Saya inginkan...** *sah-yah ee-ngin-kahn...*	
a battery	**sebiji bateri** *ser-bi-ji bah-ter-ri*	
digital prints	**cetakan digital** *cher-tah-kahn di-gi-tahl*	
a memory card	**sekeping kad memori** *ser-ker-ping kahd mey-mo-ri*	

| Can I print digital photos here? | **Bolehkah saya membuat cetakan gambar digital di sini?** *bo-ley-kah sah-yah merm-boo-aht cher-tah-kahn gahm-bar di-gi-tahl di si-ni* |

Souvenirs

a bottle of wine	**sebotol wain** *ser-bo-tol wa-ein*
a box of chocolates	**sekotak coklat** *ser-ko-tahk chok-laht*
some crystal	**beberapa Kristal** *ber-ber-ah-pah kris-tal*
a doll	**patung** *pah-toong*
some jewelry	**beberapa barang kemas** *ber-ber-ah-pah bah-rahng ker-mast*
a key ring	**cincin kunci** *chin-chin koon-chi*
a postcard	**poskad** *pos-kahd*
some pottery	**barangan tembikar** *bah-rahng-ngahn term-bi-kar*
a T-shirt	**baju kemeja-T** *bah-joo ker-mey-jah-T*
a toy	**mainan** *mah-een-nahn*
Can I see this/that?	**Boleh saya tengok ini/itu?** *Bo-ley sah-yah teh-ngok i-ni i-too?*
I'd like...	**Saya ingin...** *sah-yah ee-ngin*
a battery	**bateri** *ber-ter-ri*
a bracelet	**gelang** *ger-lahng*
a brooch	**sebentuk kerongsang** *ser-bern-took ker-rong-sahng*
a clock	**jam** *jahm*
earrings	**sepasang subang** *ser-pah-sahng soo-bahng*
a necklace	**seutas rantai** *ser-oo-tahs rahn-tai*
a ring	**sebentuk cincin** *ser-bern-took chin-chin*
a watch	**sebuah jam tangan** *ser-boo-ah jahm tah-ngahn*
I'd like...	**Saya ingin...** *sah-yah ee-ngin*
copper	**kuprum** *koo-proom*
crystal	**krystal** *krys-tahl*
diamonds	**intan** *in-tahn*

white/yellow gold	**emas putih/kuning** *er-mahs poo-tih/koo-ning*
pearls	**mutiara** *moo-ti-ah-rah*
pewter	**piuter** *pew-ter*
platinum	**platinum** *plah-ti-noom*
sterling silver	**perak tulen** *per-rak too-lern*
Is this real?	**Adakah ini asli?** *ah-dah-kah ee-ni ahs-li*
Can you engrave it?	**Bolehkah anda mengukir di atasnya?** *bo-ley-kah ahn-dah mer-ngoo-kir di ah-tahs-nyah*

Malaysia is rich in craftsmanship tradition. Typical souvenirs you will come across include silverware and pewter, hand-woven silk brocade (**kain songket**), pottery, woven mats, hats, rattan baskets, batik cloth and items of clothing, and woodcarvings.

A regular symbol of traditional craft work is the magnificent Malaysian kite known as the **wau**. A **wau** is a giant-sized kite decorated lavishly with elaborate patterns and designs. The most well-known **wau** is the **wau bulan**, which literally means 'moon kite', because it is shaped like a crescent moon adorning a full moon.

Sport & Leisure

ESSENTIAL

When's the game?	**Bilakah permainan itu?** bi-lah-kah per-mah-in-nahn ee-too
Where's the...?	**Di manakah...?** di mah-nah-kah
beach	**pantai** pahn-tai
park	**taman** tah-mahn
pool	**kolam renang** ko-lahm rer-nahng
Is it safe to swim here?	**Adakah selamat untuk berenang di sini?** ah-dah-kah ser-lah-maht oon-tuk ber-re-nahng di si-ni
Can I rent [hire] golf clubs?	**Bolehkah saya menyewa kayu golf?** bo-ley-kah sah-yah mern-nyey-wah kah-yoo golf
How much per hour?	**Berapakah bayaran untuk sejam?** ber-rah-pah-kah bah-yar-rahn oon-tuk ser-jahm
How far is it to...?	**Berapakah jauh ke...?** ber-rah-pah-kah jowh ker
Show me on the map, please.	**Sila tunjukkan kepada saya di atas peta.** si-lah toon-juk-kahn ker-pah-dah sah-yah di ah-tahs per-tah

Watching Sport

When's ... (game/race/tournament)?	**Bila... (permainan/perlumbaan/pertandingan)** Bee-lah (per-mahee-nan/per-loom-bah-ahn/per-tan-dee-ngahn?
the baseball	**besbol** beys-bol
the basketball	**bola keranjang** bo-lah ker-rahn-jahng
the boxing	**tinju** teen-joo
the cricket	**kriket** cric-ket
the cycling	**lumba basikal** Loom-bah bah-see-kal

the golf	**golf**	*golf*
the soccer [football]	**bola sepak**	*bo-lah sey-pahk*
the tennis	**tennis**	*tey-nis*
the volleyball	**bola tampar**	*bo-lah tahm-par*

Who's playing? **Siapakah yang akan bermain?** *siah-pah-kah yahng ah-kahn ber-mah-een*

Where's the racetrack/ **Di manakah litar lumba/stadium?**
stadium? *di mah-nah-kah li-tar loom-bah/stey-di-oom*

Where can I place a **Di manakah saya membuat pertaruhan?**
bet? *di mah-nah-kah sah-yah merm-boo-aht per-tah-rooh-hahn*

For Tickets, see page 19.

Silat is a form of Malaysian martial arts. Its origin is accredited to the famous Hang Tuah of old Malacca, who did not hesitate to draw his sword (**keris**), and strike to kill, for the sake of justice. Today, it is regarded as a form of exercise with artistic overtures. **Silat** displays are common at weddings and other cultural events.

Playing Sport

Where is/are...?	**Di manakah...?** *di mah-nah-kah ...*
the golf course	**padang golf** *pah-dahng golf*
the gym	**gim** *gim*
the park	**taman rekreasi** *tah-mahn rey-krey-si*
the tennis courts	**gelanggang tennis** *ger-lahng-gahng tey-nis*
How much per...	**Berapakah bayaran untuk...?** *ber-rah-pah-kah bah-yar-rahn oon-tuk ...*
day	**sehari** *ser-hah-ri*
hour	**sejam** *ser-jahm*
game	**satu permainan** *sah-too per-mah-een-nahn*
round	**satu pusingan** *sah-too poo-sing-ngahn*
Can I rent [hire]...?	**Bolehkah saya menyewa...?** *bo-ley-kah sah-yah mern-yey-wah ...*
some clubs	**kayu kah-yoo**
some equipment	**kelengkapan** *ker-lerng-kah-pahn*
a racket	**sebuah raket** *ser-boo-ah rah-keyt*
I want to go...	**Saya nak pergi...** *Sah-yah nak per-gee ...*
Caving	**kembara dalam** *gua kem-bah-ra dah-lahm gu-ah*
Diving	**Menyelam** *me-nyer-lahm*
(freshwater/ saltwater) fishing	**memancing (ikan air tawar/air masin)** *mer-mahn-cihng (ee-kahn ah-er tah-war/ah-er mah-seen)*
horseriding	**menunggang kuda** *mer-nung-gahng koo-dah*
mountain biking/ cycling	**bermotor/berbasikal digunung** *ber-mo-tor/ber-bah-see-kal di-goo-noong)*
rock climbing	**memanjat batu** *mermahn-jat bah-too*
whitewater rafting	**merakit redah jeram** *me-rah-kit rer-dah jer-ahm*
I'm a beginner.	**Saya baru belajar.** *Sah-yah bah-roo ber-lah-jar*
I'm experienced.	**Saya berpengelaman.** *Sah-yah ber-per-ngah-lah-mahn*

At the Beach/Pool

Where's the beach/pool?	**Di manakah pantai/kolam?** *di mah-nah-kah pahn-tai/koh-lahm*
Is there a…?	**Adakah …?** *ah-da-kah …*
kiddie pool	**kolam renang untuk kanak-kanak** *ko-lahm rer-nahng oon-tuk kah-nahk-kah-nahk*
indoor/outdoor pool	**kolam renang dalam rumah** *ko-lahm rer-nahng dah-lahm roo-mah*
lifeguard	**anggota penyelamat** *ahng-go-tah pern-yer-lah-maht*
Is it safe…?	**Adakah ia selamat…?** *ah-dah-kah ee-ya ser-lah-maht*
to swim	**untuk berenang** *oon-tuk ber-rer-nahng*
to dive	**untuk menyelam** *oon-tuk mern-yer-lahm*
for children	**untuk kanak-kanak** *oon-tuk kah-nahk-kah-nahk*
I'd like to hire…	**Saya ingin menyewa…** *sah-yah ee-ngin mern-yey-wah …*
a deck chair	**sebuah kerusi dek** *ser-boo-ah ker-roo-si deyk*
diving equipment	**kelengkapan menyelam** *ker-lerng-kah-pahn mern-yer-lahm*
a jet ski	**sebuah ski jet** *ser-boo-ah ski jeyt*
a motorboat	**sebuah motorbot** *ser-boo-ah mo-tor-bot*

a rowboat	**sebuah perahu dayung** *ser-boo-ah per-rah-hoo dah-yoong*
snorkeling equipment	**kelengkapan snorkel** *ker-lerng-kah-pahn snor-kerl*
a surfboard	**sebuah papan luncur air** *ser-boo-ah pah-pahn loon-choor ah-er*
a towel	**sehelai tuala** *ser-he-lai tua-lah*
an umbrella	**sekaki payung** *ser-kah-ki pah-yoong*
water skis	**ski air** *ski ah-er*
a windsurfing board	**papan luncur angin** *pah-pahn lun-cur ah-ngin*
For…hours.	**Untuk … jam.** *oon-tuk… jahm*
For the day.	**Untuk satu hari.** *Oon-tuk sah-too hah-ri*

Malaysia's rainforests are home to a variety of wildlife. The best way to see wildlife is through an acredited tour with qualified guides who know where to find the endangered orang-utans, Borneo pygmy elephants, hornbills, birds and bats. The best spots in the country are on the peninsula, Langkawi, Ulu Muda and Taman Negara, Sabah and Sarawak.

Out in the Country

A map of…, please.	**Sila berikan peta untuk…** *si-lah ber-ri-kahn per-tah oon-tuk …*
this region	**wilayah ini** *we-lah-yah ee-ni*
the walking routes	**laluan pejalan kaki** *lah-loo-an per-jah-lahn kah-ki*
the bike routes	**jalan basikal** *jah-lahn bah-si-kahl*
the trails	**jalan denai** *jah-lahn der-nai*
Is it…?	**Adakah ia…?** *ah-dah-kah ee-ya…*

easy	**mudah** *moo-dah*
difficult	**susah** *soo-sah*
far	**jauh** *jowh*
steep	**curam** *choo-rahm*
How far is it to…?	**Berapakah jauh ke…?** *ber-rah-pah-kah jowh ker …*
I'm lost.	**Saya telah sesat.** *sah-yah ter-lah ser-saht*
Where's…?	**Di manakah…?** *Di mah-nah-kah …*
the bridge	**jambatan** *jahm-bah-tahn*
the cave	**gua** *goo-ah*
the desert	**gurun** *goo-roon*
the farm	**ladang lah-dahng**
the field	**padang** *pah-dahng*
the forest	**hutan** *hoo-tahn*
the hill	**bukit** *boo-kit*
the lake	**tasik** *tah-sik*
the mountain	**gunung** *goo-noong*
the nature preserve	**hutan simpan** *hoo-tahn sim-pahn*
the viewpoint	**tempat menghayati permandangan** *term-paht merng-hah-yah-ti per-mahn-dahng-ngahn*
the park	**taman** *tah-mahn*
the path	**lorong** *lo-rong*
the peak	**puncak** *poon-chahk*
the picnic area	**tempat berkelah** *term-paht ber-key-lah*
the pond	**kolam** *ko-lahm*
the rainforest	**hutan hujan** *hoo-than hoo-jahn*
the river	**sungai** *soo-ngai*
the sea	**laut** *lah-oot*
the stream	**anak sungai** *ah-nahk soo-ngai*
the valley	**lembah** *lerm-bah*
the waterfall	**air terjun** *ah-er ter-joon*

Going Out

ESSENTIAL

What's there to do at night?	**Apakah yang boleh dibuat pada waktu malam?** *ah-pah-kah yahng bo-ley di-boo-aht pah-dah wahk-too mah-lahm*
Do you have a program of events?	**Adakah anda mempunyai senarai aturcara?** *ah-dah-kah ahn-dah merm-poon-yai ser-nah-rai ah-toor-chah-rah*
What's playing tonight?	**Apakah persembahan malam ini?** *ah-pah-kah per-serm-bah-hahn mah-lahm ee-ni*
Where's the?	**Di manakah…?** *di mah-nah-kah*
downtown area	**pusat bandar** *poo-saht bahn-dar*
bar	**bar** *bar*
dance club	**kelab menari** *ker-lahb mer-nah-ri*

Entertainment

Can you recommend…?	**Bolehkah anda mencadangkan…?** *bo-ley-kah ahn-dah mern-chah-dahng-kahn*
a concert	**sebuah konsert** *ser-boo-ah kon-sert*
a movie	**sebuah wayang gambar** *ser-boo-ah wah-yahng gahm-bar*
an opera	**sebuah opera** *ser-boo-ah o-per-rah*
a play	**sebuah pementasan drama** *ser-boo-ah per-mern-tahs-sahn drah-mah*
somewhere to see traditional dance?	**Tempat untuk menonton tarian tradisional?** *Tehm-phat oon-tuk meh-non-tone tah-ri-ahn tra-di-si-o-nal*

When does it start/ end?	**Bilakah ia bermula/tamat?** *bi-lah-kah ee-ya ber-moo-lah/tah-maht*
What's the dress code?	**Apakah cara pemakaiannya?** *ah-pah-kah chah-rah per-mah-kai-ahn-nyah*
I like…	**Saya suka…** *Sah-yah soo-kah…*
classical music	**muzik klasik** *moo-zik klah-sik*
folk music	**muzik rakyat** *moo-zik rahk-yaht*
jazz	**jaz** *jahz*
pop music	**muzik pop** *moo-kzik pop*
rap	**rap**

For Tickets, see page 19.

Authentic cultural performances can be hard to come by but classical dance troupe Temple of Fine Arts in Kuala Lumpur puts on epic productions. The best indigenous dances can be seen at longhouses, away from the big cities. In general, the best time to see any shows are during festival periods, see page 177 for more.

YOU MAY HEAR...

Sila padamkan telefon bimbit anda. *si-lah pah-dahm-kahn tey-ley-fon bim-bit ahn-dah* Turn off your mobile phones, please.

Nightlife

What's there to do at night?	**Apakah yang boleh dibuat pada waktu malam?** *ah-pah-kah yahng bo-ley di-boo-aht pah-dah wahk-too mah-lahm*
Can you recommend...?	**Bolehkah anda mencadangkan...** *bo-ley-kah ahn-dah mern-chah-dahng-kahn ...*
a bar	**sebuah bar** *ser-boo-ah bar*
a cabaret	**kabaret** *kah-bah-ret*
a casino	**sebuah kasino** *ser-boo-ah kah-si-no*
a dance club	**sebuah kelab menari** *ser-boo-ah ker-lahb mer-nah-ri*
a gay club	**kelab gay** *keh-lahb gay*
a jazz club	**sebuah kelab jaz** *ser-boo-'ah ker-lahb jahz*
a club with Malay music	**sebuah kelab dengan muzik Melayu** *ser-boo-ah ker-lahb der-ngahn moo-zik Mer-lah-yoo*

Is there live music?	**Adakah persembahan muzik langsung?**
	ah-dah-kah per-serm-bah-hahn moo-zik lahng-soong
How do I get there?	**Bagaimanakah saya boleh pergi ke sana?**
	bah-gai-mah-nah-kah sah-yah bo-ley per-gi ker sah-nah
Is there a cover charge?	**Adakah caj pintu dikenakan?** *ah-dah-kah chahj pin-*
	too di-ker-nah-kahn
Let's go dancing.	**Marilah kita pergi menari.** *mah-ri-lah ki-tah per-gi*
	mer-nar-ri
Is this area safe at	**Kawasan ni selamat ke waktu malam?**
night?	*Kah-wah-sahn ni seh-lah-mat ker wak-too mah-lam*

Pubs, clubs and karaoke lounges are where Malaysians party
at night. The best nighlife is in the capital or in hotel lounges
and bars. The dress code is quite casual but shorts and sandals are a
no-no. Local magazines such as Faces, Juice and KLue contain listings
of what's on locally and are available for free at Dome, Starbucks and
Coffee Bean & Tea Leaf outlets. Be warned, shouting and talking loudly,
even outside a nightspot, is considered rude in Malay culture and may
get you in trouble with the local authorities.

Special Requirements

ESSENTIAL

I'm here on business.	**Saya datang ke sini untuk urusan perniagaan.** *sah-yah dah-tahng ker si-ni oon-tuk oo-roo-sahn per-nee-ya-gah-ahn*
Here's my business card.	**Ini ialah kad perniagaan saya.** *ee-ni ee-ya-lah kahd per-nee-ya-gah-ahn sah-yah*
Can I have your card?	**Bolehkah saya mendapatkan kad perniagaan anda?** *bo-ley-kah sah-yah mern-dah-paht-kahn kahd per-nee-ya-gah-ahn ahn-dah*
I have a meeting with…	**Saya ada mesyuarat dengan…** *sah-yah ah-dah mer-syoo-ah-raht der-ngahn …*
Where's the…?	**Di manakah…?** *di mah-nah-kah …*
business center	**pusat perniagaan** *poo-saht per-nee-ya-gah-ahn*
convention hall	**dewan persidangan** *dey-wahn per-si-dahng-ngahn*
meeting room	**bilik mesyuarat** *bi-lik mer-syoo-ah-raht*

Seniority is much respected. It is considered rude to address older people by their names. For business associates, always use titles such as Mr, Mrs or Miss. Men should not offer to shake a Muslim lady's hand unless she offers it first. A simple nod or smile will suffice. The same can be said for women wishing to shake a Muslim man's hand.

On Business

I'm here for…	**Saya datang sini untuk…** *Sah-yah dah-tahng see-ni oon-tuk …*
a seminar	**seminar** *sem-ey-nar*

a conference	**persidangan** *per-see-dah-ngahn*
a meeting	**mesyuarat** *mer-syoo-ah-rat*
My name is…	**Nama saya ialah…** *nah-mah sah-yah ee-ya-lah …*
May I introduce my colleague…	**Benarkan saya memperkenalkan rakan sekerja saya** *ber-nah-kahn sah-yah merm-per-ker-nahl-kahn rah-kahn ser-ker-jah sah-yah*
I have a meeting/an appointment with…	**Saya ada mesyuarat/janji temu dengan…** *Sah-yah ah-dah mer-syoo-ah-rat/jahn-ji ter-moo der-ngahn…*
I'm sorry I'm late.	**Maafkan saya. Saya terlewat.** *mah-ahf-kahn sah-yah. Sah-yah ter-ley-waht*
I need an interpreter.	**Saya perlukan seorang jurubahasa.** *sah-yah per-loo-kahn ser-o-rahng joo-roo-bah-hah-sah*
You can contact me at the…Hotel.	**Anda boleh menghubungi saya di Hotel…** *ahn-dah bo-ley merng-hoo-boo-ngi sah-yah di Hotel*
I'm here until…	**Saya akan berada di sini sehingga…** *sah-yah ah-kahn ber-rah-dah di si-ni ser-hing-gah …*
I need to…	**Saya perlu…** *sah-yah per-loo …*
make a call	**membuat satu panggilan telefon** *merm-boo-aht sah-too pahng-gil-ahn tey-ley-fon*

make a photocopy	**membuat satu salinan fotokopi** *merm-boo-aht sah-too sah-lin-ahn fo-to-ko-pi*
send an e-mail	**menghantar e-mel** *merng-hahn-tah ee-mel*
send a fax	**menghantar faks** *merng-hahn-tah feyks*
send a package (for next-day delivery)	**(untuk penghantaran hari esok** *oon-tuk peng-hahn-tah-rahn hah-ri ey-sok)* **menghantar sebuah bungkusan** *merng-hahn-tah ser-boo-ah boong-koos-sahn*
It was a pleasure to meet you.	**Gembira berjumpa dengan anda.** *germ-bi-rah ber-joom-pah der-ngahn ahn-dah*

For Communications, see page 48.

YOU MAY HEAR...

Adakah anda membuat janji temu? *ah-dah-kah ahn-dah merm-boo-ahtjahn-ji ter-moo*	Do you have an appointment?
Dengan siapa? *der-ngahn siah-pah*	With whom?
Dia sedang bermesyuarat *di-ah ser-dahng ber-mer-syoo-ah-raht*	He/She is in a meeting.
Sila tunggu sekejap *si-lah toong-goo ser-ker-jahp*	One moment, please.
Dipersilakan duduk. *di-per-si-lah-kahn doo-duk*	Have a seat.
Apakah yang anda ingin minum? *ah-pah-kah yahng ahn-dah ee-ngin mi-noom*	Would you like something to drink?
Terima kasih kerana sudi datang ke sini. *ter-ri-mah kah-sih ker-rah-nah soo-di dah-tahng ker si-ni*	Thank you for coming.

Traveling with Children

ESSENTIAL

Is there a discount for kids?	**Adakah diskaun untuk kanak-kanak?** *ah-dah-kah dis-kown oon-tuk kah-nahk-kah-nahk*
Can you recommend a babysitter?	**Bolehkah anda mencadangkan seorang pengasuh kanak-kanak?** *bo-ley-kah ahn-dah mern-chah-dahng-kahn ser-o-rahng per-ngah-sooh kah-nahk-kah-nahk*
Do you have a child's seat ?	**Adakah anda ada kerusi budak?** *ah-dah-kah ahn-dah ah-dah ker-roo-si boo-dahk*
Where can I change the baby?	**Di manakah saya boleh menukar kain lampin untuk bayi?** *di mah-nah-kah bo-ley sah-yah mer-noo-kah lahm-pin oon-tuk bah-yi*

Out & About

Can you recommend something for kids?	**Bolehkah anda mencadangkan sesuatu untuk kanak-kanak?** *bo-ley-kah ahn-dah mern-chah-dahng-kahn ser-soo-ah-too oon-tuk kah-nahk-kah-nahk*
Where's…?	**Di manakah…?** *Di-mah-nah-kah…*
the amusement park	**taman hiburan** *tah-mahn hi-boor-ahn*
the arcade	**arked** *ahr-keyd*
the kiddie [paddling] pool	**kolam renang kanak-kanak** *ko-lahm rer-nahng kah-nahk-kah-nahk*
the park	**taman** *tah-mahn*
the playground	**taman permainan** *tah-mahn per-mah-een-ahn*
the zoo	**zoo** *zoo*

YOU MAY HEAR...

Begitu comel! *ber-gi-too cho-meyl*	How cute!
Apakah namanya? *ah-pah-kah nah-mah-nyah*	What's his/her name?
Berapakah umurnya? *ber-rah-pah-kah oo moor-nyah*	How old is he/she?

Are kids allowed?	**Adakah kanak-kanak dibenarkan?** *ah-dah-kah kah-nahk-kah-nahk di-ber-nah-kahn*
Is it safe for kids?	**Adakah ia selamat untuk kanak-kanak?** *ah-dah-kah ee-ya ser-lah-maht oon-tuk kah-nahk-kah-nahk*
Is it suitable for... year olds?	**Adakah ia sesuai untuk kanak-kanak berumur...?** *ah-dah-kah ee-ya ser-soo-ai oon-tuk kah-nahk-kah-nahk ber-roo-moor ...*

For Numbers, see page 153.

The Malay greeting (**salam**) involves brushing the palm of the other person and placing the hand on one's heart. This signifies "I am pleased to meet you from the bottom of my heart."

Baby Essentials

Do you have...?	**Adakah anda mempunyai...?** *ah-dah-kah ahn-dah merm-poon-ya ...*
a baby bottle	**botol bayi** *bo-tol bah-yi*
baby food	**makanan bayi** *mah-kahn-nahn bah-yi*
baby wipes	**tisu lembap untuk bayi** *ti-soo lerm-bahp oon-tuk bah-yi*

a car seat	**kerusi kereta budak** *ker-roo-si ker-rey-tah boo-dahk*
a children's menu/ portion	**menu/bahagian untuk kanak-kanak** *mey-noo/bah-hah-gi-ahn oon-tuk kah-nahk-kah-nahk*
a child's seat/ highchair	**kerusi budak/tinggi budak** *ker-roo-si boo-dahk/ ting-gi boo-dahk*
a crib/cot	**katil bayi** *kah-til bah-yi*
diapers [nappies]	**kain lampin bayi** *kah-een lahm-pin bah-yi*
formula	**susu bayi** *soo-soo bah-yi*
a pacifier [dummy]	**puting** *poo-ting*
a playpen	**kandang main** *kahn-dahng mah-een*
a stroller [pushchair]	**kereta sorong bayi** *ker-rey-tah so-rong bah-yi*
Can I breastfeed the baby here?	**Bolehkah saya menyusu bayi di sini?** *bo-ley-kah sah-yah mer-nyoo-soo bah-yi di si-ni*
Where can I breastfeed/ change the baby?	**Di mana saya boleh menyusukan/menyalin bayi?** *Di-mah-nah sah-yah bo-ley meh-nyoo-soo-kahn bah-yee*

Malaysian infrastructure is not particularly baby-friendly, even in the cities. There are few mothers' rooms or nappy-changing tables in toilets, and it may be difficult to buy infant products in rural areas. Public transport and public areas are unsympathetic to pushchairs. However, a helping hand is never far away. Children under 12 travel for half-price on buses and boats.

Babysitting

| Can you recommend a babysitter? | **Bolehkah anda mencadangkan seorang pengasuh kanak-kanak?** *bo-ley-kah ahn-dah mern-chah-dahng-kahn ser-o-rahng per-ngah-sooh kah-nahk-kah-nahk* |

How much do you/ they charge?	**Berapakah bayaran yang dikenakan?** *ber-rah-pah-kah bah-yah-rahn yahng di-ker-nah-kahn*
I'll be back at…	**Saya akan pulang sebelum…** *sah-yah ah-kahn poo-lahng pah-dah*
If you need to contact me, call…	**Kalau awak perlu menghubungi saya, telefon…** *Kah-lau ah-wak per-loo meng-hoo-boo-ngi sah-yah, te-le-fon…*

For Time, see page 175.

Health & Emergency

Can you recommend a pediatrician?	**Bolehkah anda mencadangkan seorang doktor pakar kanak-kanak?** *bo-ley-kah ahn-dah mern-chah-dahng-kahn ser-o-rahng dok-tor pah-kah kah-nahk-kah-nahk*
My child is allergic to…	**Anak saya alah pada…** *ah-nahk sah-yah ah-lah pah-dah*
My child is missing.	**Anak saya telah hilang.** *ah-nahk sah-yah ter-lah hi-lahng*
Have you seen a boy/girl?	**Adakah anda ternampak seorang budak lelaki/ perempuan?** *ah-dah-kah ahn-dah ter-nahm-pahk ser-o-rahng boo-dahk ler-lah-ki/per-rerm-poo-ahn*

For Police, see page 156.

Disabled Travelers

ESSENTIAL

Is there...?	**Adakah...** *ah-dah-kah ...*
access for the disabled	**jalan masuk untuk orang kurang upaya?** *jah-lahn mah-suk oon-tuk o-rahng koo-rahng oo-pah-yah*
a wheelchair ramp	**tanjakan untuk kerusi roda** *tahn-jahk-ahn oon-tuk ker-roo-si ro-dah*
a handicapped [disabled-] accessible toilet	**tandas mesra orang kurang upaya** *tahn-dahs mers-rah o-rahng koo-rahng oo-pah-yah*
I need...	**Saya memerlukan...** *sah-yah mer-mer-loo-kahn*
assistance	**bantuan** *bahn-too-ahn*
an elevator [a lift]	**sebuah lif** *ser-boo-ah lif*
a ground-floor room	**sebuah bilik tingkat bawah** *ser-boo-ah bi-lik ting-kaht bah-wah*

Asking for Assistance

I'm...	**Sa-ya...** *sah-yah ...*
disabled	**kurang upaya** *koo-rahng oo-pah-yah*
visually impaired	**cacat penglihatan** *chah-chaht perng-li-haht-tahn*
deaf	**pekak** *per-kahk*
hearing impaired	**cacat pendengaran** *chah-chaht pern-der-ngah-rahn*
unable to walk far/ use the stairs	**tidak boleh berjalan jauh/menggunakan tangga** *ti-dahk bo-ley ber-jah-lahn jah-ooh/ merng-goo-nah-kahn tahng-gah*
Please speak louder.	**Sila bercakap dengan lebih kuat.** *si-lah ber-chah-kahp der-ngahn ler-bih koo-aht*

Can I bring my wheelchair?	**Bolehkah saya membawa kerusi roda saya?** *bo-ley-kah sah-yah merm-bah-wah ker-roo-si ro-dah sah-yah*
Are guide dogs permitted?	**Adakah anjing pemandu dibenarkan?** *ah-dah-kah ahn-jing per-mahn-doo di-ber-nah-kahn*
Can you help me?	**Bolehkah anda menolong saya?** *bo-ley-kah ahn-dah mer-no-long sah-yah*
Please open/hold the door.	**Sila buka/pegang pintu itu.** *si-lah boo-kah/ per-gahng pin-too ee-too*

For Health, see page 158.

Malaysia's major hotels, malls, theatres, fast-food chains and some government buildings in the bigger cities all have wheelchair ramps and disabled-accessible toilets, and extra-wide parking bays. KL International Airport and Light rail transit (LRT) system are also well equipped. However, outside of these cities, the streets are often uneven and difficult to navigate. Taxis will not usually transport people in wheelchairs or will apply additional charges.

In an Emergency

Emergencies

ESSENTIAL

Help!	**Tolong!** *to-long*
Go away!	**Pergi!** *per-gi*
Stop, thief!	**Berhenti, pencuri!** *ber-hern-ti pern-choo-ri*
Get a doctor!	**Dapatkan doktor!** *dah-paht-kahn dok-tor*
Fire!	**Api!** *ah-pi*
I'm lost.	**Saya tersesat.** *sah-yah ter-ser-saht*
Can you help me?	**Bolehkah anda membantu saya?**
	bo-ley-kah ahn-dah merm-bahn-too sah-yah

In an emergency, dial 999 for the police, ambulance or the fire department. Is using a cell [mobile] phone, dial 112.

YOU MAY HEAR...

Isikan borang ini. *ee-si-kahn bo-rahng ee-ni*	Fill out this form.
Sila tunjukkan kad pengenalan anda.	Your identification, please.
si-lah toon-juk-kahn kahd per-nger-nah-lahn	
ahn-dah	
Bilakah/Di manakah ia berlaku?	When/Where did it
bi-lah-kah/di mah-nah-kah ee-ya ber-lah-koo	happen?
Bagaimanakah rupa lelaki/ perempuan itu?	What does he/she look
bah-gai-mah-nah-kah roo-pah ler-lah-ki/	like?
per-rerm-poo-ahn ee-tu	

Police

ESSENTIAL

Call the police!	**Panggil polis!** *pahng-gil po-lis*
Where's the police station?	**Di manakah balai polis?** *di mah-nah-kah bah-lai po-lis*
There was an accident/attack.	**Satu kemalangan/serangan berlaku tadi.** *sah-too ker-mah-lah-ngahn/ser-rah-ngahn ber-lah-koo tah-di*
My child is missing.	**Anak saya telah hilang.** *ah-nahk sah-yah ter-lah hi-lahng*
I need...	**Saya perlu...** *sah-yah per-loo...*
an interpreter	**seorang jurubahasa** *ser-o-rahng joo-roo-bah-hah-sah*
to contact my lawyer	**menghubungi peguam saya** *merng-hoo-boo-ngi per-goo-ahm sah-yah*
to make a phone call.	**membuat satu panggilan telefon** *merm-boo-aht sah-too pahng-gil-ahn tey-ley-fon*
I'm innocent.	**Saya tidak bersalah.** *sah-yah ti-dahk ber-sah-lah*

Crime & Lost Property

I want to report...	**Saya mahu melaporkan...** *Sah-yah mah-hoo mer-lah-por-kahn ...*
a mugging	**samun** *sah-moon*
a rape	**rogol** *row-gol*
a theft	**kecurian** *ker-coo-ri-ahn*
I was mugged.	**Saya disamun.** *Sah-yah di-sah-moon*
I was robbed.	**Saya dirompak.** *Sah-yah di-rhom-pak*

I lost…	**Saya hilang…** *Sah-yah hee-lahng…*
…was stolen.	**…telah dicuri** *…ter-lah di-coo-ri*
My backpack	**Beg galas saya** *Beg- gah-las sah-yah*
My bicycle	**Basikal saya** *Bah-see-kal sah-yah*
My camera	**Kamera saya** *Kah-meh-rah sah-yah*
My (hire) car	**Kereta (sewa) saya** *Ker-ray-tah (say-wah) sah-yah*
My computer	**Komputer saya** *Kom-poo-ter sah-yah*
My credit card	**Kad kredit saya** *Kat-kray-dit sah-yah*
My jewelry	**Barang kemas saya** *Bah-rahng ker-mast sah-yah*
My money	**Duit saya** *Doo-it sah-yah*
My passport	**Pasport saya** *Pas-port sah-yah*
My purse [handbag]	**Beg duit (beg tangan) saya** *Beyg doo-it (beyg tah-ngahn) sah-yah*
My traveler's cheques	**Cek pengembara saya** *Chek- per-ngem-bah-rah sah-yah*
My wallet	**Dompet saya** *Dome-pet sah-yah*
I need a police report.	**Saya perlukan laporan polis.** *sah-yah per-loo-kan lah-po-rahn poh-lis.*
Where is the British/ American/Irish embassy?	**Di manakah kedutaan British/Amerika/Ireland?** *Di-mah-nah-kah ker-doo-tah-ahn British/Amerika/ Ireland?*

Health

ESSENTIAL

I'm sick.	**Saya sakit.** *sah-yah sah-kit*
I need an English-speaking doctor.	**Saya perlu seorang doktor yang bercakap Bahasa Inggeris.** *sah-yah per-loo ser-o-rahng dok-tor yahng ber-chah-kahp Bah-hah-sah Ing-ger-ris*
It hurts here.	**Sakit di sini.** *sah-kit di si-ni*
I have a stomach ache.	**Perut saya sakit.** *per-root sah-yah sah-kit*

The water in cities is generally safe for drinking, but it is best to boil it first. Bottled drinks are widely available. Avoid drinking iced water from roadside stalls. It is important to drink sufficiently to avoid dehydration; drink more than you would normally if you are from a temperate country. Cooked food from most stalls is generally safe. If you are visiting remote rainforest areas, it is advisable to take protection against malaria. See your doctor before leaving home. Malaria tablets are only available on prescription in Malaysia.

Finding a Doctor

Can you recommend a doctor/dentist?	**Bolehkah anda mencadangkan seorang doktor/ doktor gigi?** *bo-ley-kah ahn-dah mern-chah-dahng-kahn ser-o-rahng dok-tor/dok-tor gi-g*
Can the doctor	**Bolehkah doktor itu datang ke sini?** *bo-ley-kah dok-tor ee-too dah-tahng ker si-ni*
I need an English-speaking doctor.	**Saya perlu seorang doktor yang bercakap Bahasa Inggeris.** *sah-yah per-loo ser-o-rahng dok-tor yahng ber-chah-kahp Bah-hah-sah Ing-ger-ris*

What are the office hours?	**Apakah waktu pejabatnya?** *ah-pah-kah wahk-too per-jah-baht-nyah*
I'd like an appointment for...	**Saya ingin membuat janji temu untuk...** *sah-yah ee-ngin merm-boo-aht jahn-ji ter-moo oon-tuk*
today	**hari ini** *hah-ri ee-ni*
tomorrow	**esok** *ey-sok*
as soon as possible	**secepat mungkin** *ser-cer-paht moong-kin*
It's urgent.	**Ia sangat penting.** *ee-ya sah-ngaht pern-ting*

Symptoms

I'm bleeding.	**Saya luka berdarah.** *sah-yah loo-kah ber-dah-rah.*
I'm constipated.	**Saya sembelit.** *sah-yah sem-ber-lit.*
I'm dizzy.	**Saya pening.** *sah-yah per-nihng*
I'm nauseous.	**Saya rasa mual.** *sah-yah rah-sah moo-al*
I'm vomiting.	**Saya muntah.** *sah-yah moon-tah*
It hurts here.	**Sakit di sini.** *sah-kit di si-ni*
I have...	**Saya...** *sah-yah...*
an allergic reaction	**ada alahan** *ah-dah ar-lah-hahn*
chest pain	**sakit dada** *sah kit dah-dah*
cramps	**kekejangan** *ker-ker-jar-ngahn*
diarrhea	**cirit-birit** *cee-rit bee-rit*

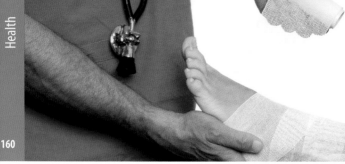

an earache	**sakit telinga** *sah-kit ter-lee-ngah*
a fever	**demam** *der-mam*
pain	**sakit** *sah-kit*
a rash	**ruam** *roo-ahm*
a sprain	**terseliuh** *ter-ser-lee-uh*
some swelling	**ada bengkak sikit** *ah-dah behng-kak si-kit*
a sore throat	**sakit tekak** *sah-kit ter-lee-ngah*
a stomachache	**sakit perut** *sah-kit per-root*
I've been sick	**Saya dah sakit** *Sah-yah dah sah-kit*
for...days.	**Selama...hari.** *Ser-lah-mah...hah-ree*

For Numbers, see page 173.

Conditions

I'm...	**Saya...** *Sah-yah ...*
anemic	**anemik** *a-ner-mik*
asthmatic	**lelah** *ler-lah*
diabetic	**kencing manis** *khen-cihng man-is*
epileptic	**epilepsi** *er-pi-lep-si*
I'm allergic to	**Saya alah pada** *Sah-yah ar-lah pah-dah*
antibiotics	**antibiotic** *an-ti-bio-tik*
penicillin	**Penisilin** *pen-ey-cil-an*

YOU MAY HEAR...

Apakah masalahnya?   What's wrong?
ah-pah-kah mah-sah-lah-nyah

Sakitnya di mana? *sah-kit-nyah di mah-nah*   Where does it hurt?

Adakah ia sakit di sini?   Does it hurt here?
ah-dah-kah ee-ya sah-kit di si-ni

Adakah anda sedang makan ubat?   Are you on medication?
ah-dah-kah ahn-dah ser-dahng mah-kahn oo-baht

Adakah anda alah terhadap apa-apa?   Are you allergic to
ah-dah-kah ahn-dah ah-lah   anything?
ter-hah-dahp ah-pah-ah-pah

Apakah masalahnya?   What's wrong?
ah-pah-kah mah-sah-lah-nyah

Buka mulut anda. *boo-kah moo-loot ahn-dah*   Open your mouth.

Tarik nafas. *tah-rik nah-fahs*   Breathe deeply.

Sila batuk. *si-lah bah-took*   Cough please.

Pergi ke hospital. *per-gi ker hos-pi-tahl*   Go to the hospital.

Ia... *ee-yah ...*   It's...

telah patah *ter-lah pah-tah*   broken

boleh berjangkit *bo-ley ber-jahng-kit*   contagious

telah dijangkiti kuman   infected
ter-lah di-jahng-ki-ti koo-mahn

terseliuh *ter-ser-li-ooh*   sprained

tidak serius *ti-dahk ser-ri-oos*   nothing serious

I have...	**Saya ada...** *Sah-yah ah-dah ...*
arthritis	**artritis** *ar-tri-tis*
a heart condition	**masalah jantung** *mah-sah-lah jahn-toong*

| high/low blood pressure | **tekanan darah tinggi/rendah** *ter-kah-nahn dah-rah ting-gi/ren-dah* |
| I'm on… | **Saya sedang mengambil…** *Sah-yah ser-dang mer-ngam-bil…* |

For Meals & Cooking, see page 72.

Treatment

Do I need a prescription/medicine?	**Saya perlukan preskripsi/ubat ke?** *Sah-yah per-loo-kahn pres-krip-si/oo-bat ker?*
Can you prescribe a generic drug?	**Boleh awak berikan ubat biasa?** *Bo-ley ah-wak ber-ee-kahn oo-bat bi-ah-sah?*
Where can I get it?	**Di mana saya boleh dapatkannya?** *Di-mah-nah-kah sah-yah bo-ley dah-pat-kahn-nya?*

For What to Take, see page 165.

Hospital

Notify my family, please.	**Sila hubungi keluarga saya.** *si-lah hoo-boo-ngi ker-loo-ah-gah sah-yah*
I'm in pain.	**Saya dalam kesakitan.** *sah-yah dah-lahm ker-sah-kit-ahn*
I need a doctor/nurse.	**Saya perlu seorang doktor/jururawat.** *sah-yah per-loo ser-o-rahng dok-tor/joo-roo-rah-waht*
When are visiting hours?	**Bilakah waktu melawat?** *bi-lah-kah wahk-too mer-lah-waht*
I'm visiting…	**Saya sedang melawat…** *sah-yah ser-dahng mer-lah-waht …*

Dentist

I have…	**Saya dah…** *Sah-yah dah …*
a broken tooth	**patah gigi** *pah-tah gee-gee*
a lost filling	**hilang tampalan gigi** *hee-lahng tam-pah-lahn gee-gee*

a toothache	**sakit gigi** *sah-kit gee-gee*
Can you fix this denture?	**Boleh awak betulkan gigi palsu ini?** *Bo-ley ah-wak ber-tol-kahn gee-gee pal-soo ee-ni?*

Gynecologist

I have cramps/ a vaginal infection.	**Saya terkena kekejangan/jangkitan faraj.** *sah-yah ter-ker-nah ker-ker-jang-ahn /jang-kee-tan fah-raj.*
I missed my period.	**Haid saya tak datang.** *hah-eed sah-yah tak dah-tahng*
I'm on the Pill.	**Saya mengambil Pil Perancang.** *sah-yah meng-ahm-bil Pil Per-rahn-cahng*
I'm (...months) pregnant.	**Saya mengandung (...bulan)** *sah-yah me-ngahn-doong (....boo-lan)*
I'm not pregnant.	**Saya tak mengandung.** *sah-yah tak me-ngahn-doong*
My last period was...	**Haid saya yang terakhir pada...** *hah-eed sah-yahng ter-ah-heer...*

For Numbers, see page 173.

Optician

I lost...	**Saya hilang...** *sah-yah hee-lahng...*
a contact lens	**kanta sentuh** *kahn-tah sen-tuh*
my glasses	**kaca mata saya** *kah-cah mah-tah sah-yah*
a lens	**lensa** *len-sah*

Payment & Insurance

How much?	**Berapakah harganya?** *ber-rah-pah-kah har-gah-nyah*
Can I pay by credit card?	**Bolehkah saya bayar dengan kad kredit?** *bo-ley-kah sah-yah bah-yah der-ngahn kahd krey-dit*
I have insurance.	**Saya ada insurans.** *sah-yah ah-dah in-soo-rahns*
I need a receipt for my insurance.	**Saya perlukan resit untuk insurans saya.** *sah-yah per-loo-kahn rer-sit oon-tuk in-soo-rahns sah-ya.*

Pharmacy

ESSENTIAL

Where's the pharmacy?	**Di manakah farmasi?** *di mah-nah-kah fah-mah-si*
What time does it open/close?	**Pukul berapakah ia akan dibuka/ditutup?** *poo-kool ber-rah-pah-kah ee-ya ah-kahn di-boo-kah/ di-too-tup*
What would you recommend for...?	**Apakah yang akan anda cadangkan untuk...?** *ah-pah-kah yahng ah-kahn ahn-dah chah-dahng-kahn oon-tuk ...*
How much do I take?	**Berapakah yang patut saya ambil?** *ber-rah-pah-kah yahng pah-toot sah-yah ahm-bil*
Can you fill [up] this prescription?	**Bolehkah anda penuhi preskripsi ini?** *bo-ley-kah ahn-dah per-noo-hee pre-skrip-si ee-ni*
I'm allergic to...	**Saya alah kepada...** *sah-yah ah-lah ker-pah-dah*

Most shopping malls have pharmacies operated by chains such as Watson's, Georgetown Caring, Vitacare and Guardian. For 24-hour services, try one of the polyclinics or private clinics. They are quite likely to have English-speaking staff and they dispense most generic medicines.

What to Take

How much do I take?	**Berapa banyak perlu saya ambil?** *Ber-ah-pah bah-nyak per-loo sah-yah ahm-bil*
How often?	**Berapa kerap?** *ber-ah-pah ker-rapt?*
Is it safe for children?	**Adakah ia selamat untuk kanak-kanak?** *ah-dah-kah ee-ar ser-lah-mat oon-tuk kah-nak-kah-nak*
I'm taking...	**Saya sedang ambil...** *sah-yah ser-dahng ahm-bil...*
Are there side effects?	**Ada apa-apa kesan sampingan?** *Ah-dah ah-pah-ah-pah ker-sahn sam-pee-ngahn*
I need something for...	**Saya perlukan sesuatu untuk...** *sah-yah per-loo-kahn ser-soo-ah-too oon-tuk...*
a cold	**selsema** *serl-ser-mah*

a cough	**batuk** bah-took
diarrhea	**cirit-birit** chi-rit-bi-rit
a fever	**demam** der-mahm
a headache	**sakit kepala** sah-kit ker-pah-lah
insect bites	**gigitan serangga** gi-gi-tahn ser-rahng-gah
motion sickness	**mabuk perjalanan** mah-book per-jah-lah-nan
a sore throat	**sakit tekak** sah-kit ter-kak
sunburn	**selaran matahari** ser-lah-rahn mah-tah-hah-ri
a toothache	**sakit gigi** sah-kit gee-gee
an upset stomach	**sakit perut** sah-kit per-root

YOU MAY SEE...

SEKALI/TIGA KALI SEHARI	once/three times a day
PIL	tablet
TITIK	drop
SUDU KECIL	teaspoon
...MAKAN	...meals
SELEPAS	After
SEBELUM	Before
DENGAN	With
DENGAN PERUT YANG KOSONG	on an empty stomach
TELAN SEGALANYA	swallow whole
BOLEH MENYEBABKAN KEPENINGAN	may cause drowsiness
JANGAN MAKAN	do not ingest

Basic Supplies

I'd like...	**Saya inginkan...** sah-yah ee-ngin-kahn...
acetaminophen [paracetamol]	**panadol** pah-nah-dol
antiseptic cream	**losen selepas bercukur** lo-syeyn ser-ler-pahs ber-choo-koor

aspirin	**aspirin** *ahs-pi-rin*	
Band Aid [plasters]	**Band Aid [plasters]** *band-aid [pla-sters]*	
bandages	**pembalut luka** *perm-bah-loot loo-kah*	
a comb	**sikat** *si-kaht*	
condoms	**kondom** *kon-dom*	
contact lens solution	**cecair pencuci kanta sentuh** *cher-chah-ir pern-choo-chi kahn-tah sern-tooh*	
deodorant	**deodoran** *deo-do-rahn*	
a hairbrush	**berus rambut** *ber-roos rahm-boot*	
hairspray	**penyembur rambut** *pern-yerm-boor rahm-boot*	
ibuprofen	**ibuprofen** *ee-boo-pro-fern*	
insect repellent	**penghalau serangga** *perng-hah-lau ser-rahng-gah*	
lotion	**losen** *lo-seyn*	
a nail file	**kikir kuku** *ki-kir koo-koo*	
a (disposable) razor	**pencukur (pakai buang)** *pern-choo-koor (pah-kah-ee boo-ahng)*	
razor blades	**pisau pencukur** *pi-sow pern-choo-koor*	
sanitary napkins [pads]	**tuala wanita** *too-ah-lah wah-ni-tah*	
a scissors	**gunting** *goon-ting*	
shampoo/ conditioner	**syampu/perapi** *syahm-poo/per-rah-pi*	
soap	**sabun** *sah-boon*	
sunscreen	**losen pelindung matahari** *lo-seyn per-lin-doong mah-tah-hah-ri*	
tampons	**tampon** *tahm-pon*	
tissues	**tisu** *ti-soo*	
toilet paper	**kertas tandas** *ker-tahs tahn-dahs*	
toothpaste	**ubat gigi** *oo-baht gi-gi*	

For Baby Essentials, see page 149.

The Basics

Grammar

Word order in Malay is usually the same as in English: subject, verb, object. The Malay language is made up of root words, and inflected words formed by adding prefixes and suffixes to the root word. These affixations change the nature of the root word, turning the word from a noun/adjective/verb to a verb or an abstract noun. Sometimes, the affixations change the meaning of the word completely.

Verbs

Affixations such as **ber-**, **ber – an**, **ber – kan**, **men**, **– kan** **memper – kan** or **memper – i** are used to make verbs.
For example:

walk	**jalan**;
to walk	**berjalan**;
to implement	**menjalankan**

Malay verbs do not have singular or plural forms. They also do not have present, past or future tenses. Instead, there is one basic verb form that is used for every person and time.

Actions at different times are usually expressed using adverbs of time such as yesterday, tomorrow, etc. Time can also be expressed by using the word **telah**. It is used to show an action had been done previously:

I have eaten.	**Saya telah makan.** *sah-yah ter-lah mah-kahn*
I had breakfast.	**Saya telah makan sarapan pagi.**
	sah-yah ter-lah mah-kahn sah-rah-pahn pah-gi

To show that an action is still ongoing, use **sedang**:

I am eating a mango.	**Saya sedang makan sebiji mempelam.** *sah-yah ser-dahng mah-kahn ser-bi-ji merm-per-lahm kan*

The suffix **-kan** is used to form a passive verb, showing causation or transitivity:

beri – give; **berikan** – give (me)

Personal Pronouns

I	**saya** *sah-yah*
you	**kamu/anda** *kah-moo/ahn-dah*
he/she	**dia** *di-ah*
it	**ia** *ee-ya*
we	**kami** *kah-mi*
you	**kamu/anda** *kah-moo/ahn-dah*
they	**mereka** *mer-rey-kah*

Note that in Malay, there is no differentiation in the gender of pronouns. Personal pronouns also do not require different verb forms:

I am	**Saya ialah** *sah-yah ee-ya-lah*
He is	**Dia ialah** *di-ah ee-ya-lah*
They are	**Mereka ialah** *mer-rey-kah ee-ya-lah*

To make a pronoun possessive, just add the pronoun behind the subject:

My passport.	**Pasport saya** *pahs-port sah-yah*
Their bags.	**Beg-beg mereka** *beyg-beyg mer-rey-kah*

Nouns & Adjectives

Like in English, there are concrete and abstract nouns in Malay. Concrete nouns are objects that can be seen, held and felt, while abstract nouns are intangible. The affix **ke-an** is used to turn a root word into an abstract noun:

e.g. **bersih** – clean   **kebersihan** – cleanliness

Some nouns are formed by adding prefixes and suffixes to the root word:

e.g. pretty (adj)   **cantik**
beauty (noun, thing)   **kecantikan** ('ke + an' affixation)
rob (verb)   **rompak**
robber (noun, person)   **perompak** ('pe-' affixation)
robbery (noun, thing)   **perompakan** ('pe + an' affixation)

Plurals can be formed by repeating the noun.

My bag is missing.	**Beg saya telah hilang.** *beyg sah-yah ter-lah hee-lahng*
My bags are missing.	**Beg-beg saya telah hilang.** *beyg-beyg sah-yah ter-lah hee-lahng*

Questions

Questions are usually formed using these question words:
who – **siapa**; what – **apa**; when – **bila**; which – **yang mana**;
where – **di mana**; how – **bagaimana**
how much? **berapa**

For Example:

What is that?	**Itu apa?** *ee-too ah-pah*
How much is that?	**Itu berapa?** *ee-too ber-rah-pah*
Where are you from?	**Anda dari mana?** *ahn-dah dah-ri mah-nah*
For whom?	**Untuk siapa?** *oon-tuk siah-pah*

Adjectives

Unlike English, adjectives come after nouns in Malay. Adjectives with two or more syllables usually have the word **yang** preceding the adjective:
For example:

a tasty dish   **hidangan yang sedap**
hi-dah-ngahn yahng ser-dahp

a mesmerizing scenery   **pemandangan yang menawan**
per-mahn-dah-ngahn yahng mer-nah-wahn

Collective Nouns

Here are some commonly used collective nouns and examples of their usage.

1. **batang** – used for things that are long, such as a tree, a pen, a river, etc.

| Can I have a pen? | **Bolehkah berikan saya sebatang pen?**
bo-ley-kah ber-ri-kahn sah-yah ser-bah-tahng peyn |

The prefix '**se-**' is added to the collective noun to signify 'one'.
If the number is more than one, just add the number in front.

| Can I have two pens? | **Bolehkah berikan saya dua batang pen?**
bo-ley-kah ber-ri-kahn sah-yah doo-ah bah-tahng peyn |

2. **bentuk** – used for things with curves, such as a ring and the fishing hook.

| I would like to get a ring as a gift. | **Saya ingin membeli sebentuk cincin sebagai hadiah.** *sah-yah ee-ngin merm-ber-li ser-bern-took chin-chin ser-bah-gai hah-diah* |

3. **biji** – used for small rounded things, such as eggs, fruits and others.

| I have bought three eggs, a pineapple and five oranges. | **Saya telah membeli tiga biji telur, sebiji nanas dan lima biji oren.** *sah-yah ter-lah merm-ber-li ti-gah bi-ji ter-loor, ser-bi-ji nah-nahs dahn li-mah bi-ji o-reyn* |

4. **keping** – used for things that are flat and thin, such as a photograph, a piece of bread, a piece of wood and others.

| I would like to send a postcard to my family. | **Saya ingin menghantar sekeping poskad kepada keluarga saya.** *sah-yah ee-ngin merng-hahn-tah ser-ker-ping pos-kahd ker-pah-dah ker-loo-ah-gah sah-yah* |

Prepositions

The most common prepositions are **dari**, **daripada**, **di** and **ke**:

dari – from (a place)

| I am from London. | **Saya dari London**. *sah-yah dar-ee Lon-don* |

daripada – from (whom)

| I bought these handicrafts from the old lady by the roadside. | **Saya membeli barangan kraftangan ini daripada nenek tua yang menjaja di tepi jalan.** *sah-yah mem-bel-ee bar-an-gan kraf-tan-gan ee-ni dar-ee-pa-dah ne-nek too-ah yang men-ja-ja di te-pee jah-lan* |

di – at

| ...at the hotel. | **...di hotel.** *hi ho-tel* |

ke – to

| I am going to the zoo. | **Saya akan pergi ke zoo**. *sah-yah ah-khan per-gi kee zoo* |

Adverbs

Adverbs in Malay are usually followed by **dengan** and precede the verbs they modify. For example:

| work carefully | **bekerja dengan berhati-hati** *ber-ker-jah der-ngahn ber-hah-ti-hah-ti* |
| drive carefully | **pandu dengan cermat/pandu cermat** *pahn-doo der-ngahn cher-maht/pahn-doo cher-maht* |

Note that in some instances, the word **dengan** can be dropped:

Negation

Tidak (no) or **bukan** (not) is added before the verb to indicate negation.E.g.

| Would you like tea? | **Adakah anda ingin minum teh?** *ah-dah-kah ahn-dah ee-ngin mi-noom teyh* |
| No. | **Tidak.** *ti-dahk* |

More examples:

Am not	**bukan** *boo-kahn*
Have not	**belum** *ber-loom*
Cannot	**tidak boleh** *ti-dahk bo-ley*
I am not on vacation.	**Saya bukan sedang bercuti.** *sah-yah boo-kahn ser-dahng ber-choo-ti*
I have not bought the ticket.	**Saya belum membeli tiket.** *sah-yah ber-loom merm-ber-li ti-keyt*
I cannot take milk.	**Saya tidak boleh minum susu.** *sah-yah ti-dahk bo-ley mi-noom soo-soo*

Numbers

ESSENTIAL

0	**sifa** *si-fah*
1	**satu** *sah-too*
2	**dua** *doo-ah*
3	**tiga** *ti-gah*
4	**empat** *erm-paht*
5	**lima** *li-mah*
6	**enam** *er-nahm*
7	**tujuh** *too-jooh*
8	**lapan** *lah-pahn*
9	**sembilan** *serm-bi-lahn*

10	**sepuluh**	*ser-poo-looh*
11	**sebelas**	*ser-ber-lahs*
12	**dua belas**	*doo-ah ber-lahs*
13	**tiga belas**	*ti-gah ber-lahs*
14	**empat belas**	*erm-paht ber-lahs*
15	**lima belas**	*li-mah ber-lahs*
16	**enam belas**	*er-nahm ber-lahs*
17	**tujuh belas**	*too-jooh ber-lahs*
18	**lapan belas**	*lah-pahn ber-lahs*
19	**sembilan belas**	*serm-bi-lahn ber-lahs*
20	**dua puluh**	*doo-ah poo-looh*
21	**dua puluh satu**	*doo-ah poo-looh sah-too*
22	**dua puluh dua**	*doo-ah poo-looh doo-ah*
30	**tiga puluh**	*ti-gah poo-looh*
31	**tiga puluh satu**	*ti-gah poo-looh sah-too*
40	**empat puluh**	*erm-paht poo-looh*
50	**lima puluh**	*li-mah poo-looh*
60	**enam puluh**	*er-nahm poo-looh*
70	**tujuh puluh**	*too-jooh poo-looh*
80	**lapan puluh**	*lah-pahn poo-looh*
90	**sembilan puluh**	*serm-bi-lahn poo-looh*
100	**seratus**	*ser-rah-toos*
101	**seratus satu**	*ser-rah-toos sah-too*
200	**dua ratus**	*doo-ah rah-toos*
500	**lima ratus**	*li-mah rah-toos*
1,000	**seribu**	*ser-ri-boo*
10,000	**sepuluh ribu**	*ser-poo-looh ri-boo*
100,000	**seratus ribu**	*ser-rah-toos ri-boo*
1,000,000	**satu juta**	*sah-too joo-tah*

Ordinal Numbers

first	**pertama**	*per-tah-mah*
second	**kedua**	*ker-doo-ah*
third	**ketiga**	*ker-ti-gah*
fourth	**keempat**	*ker-erm-paht*
fifth	**kelima**	*ker-li-mah*
once	**sekali**	*ser-kah-li*
twice	**dua kali**	*doo-ah kah-li*
three times	**tiga kali**	*ti-gah kah-li*

Time

ESSENTIAL

What time is it?	**Pukul berapa?** *poo-kool ber-rah-pah*
It's midday.	**Sekarang waktu tengahari.** *ser-kah-rahng wahk-too ter-ngah-hah-ri*
At midnight.	**Pada waktu tengah malam.** *pah-dah wahk-too ter-ngah mah-lahm*
From one o'clock to two o'clock.	**Dari pukul satu hingga pukul dua.** *dah-ri poo-kool sah-too hing-gah poo-kool doo-ah*
Five past three.	**Pukul tiga kosong lima.** *poo-kool ti-gah ko-song li-mah*
A quarter to ten.	**Pukul tiga empat puluh lima.** *poo-kool ti-gah erm-paht poo-looh li-mah*
5:30 a.m./p.m.	**5:30 pagi/petang.** *5:30 pah-gi/per-tahng*

Days

ESSENTIAL

Monday	**Isnin** *Is-nin*
Tuesday	**Selasa** *Ser-lah-sah*
Wednesday	**Rabu** *Rah-boo*
Thursday	**Khamis** *Khah-mis*
Friday	**Jumaat** *Joo-mah-aht*
Saturday	**Sabtu** *Sahb-too*
Sunday	**Ahad** *Ah-hahd*

Dates

yesterday	**kelmarin** *kerl-mah-rin*
today	**hari ini** *hah-ri ee-ni*
tomorrow	**esok** *ey-sok*
day	**hari** *hah-ri*
week	**minggu** *ming-goo*
month	**bulan** *boo-lahn*
year	**tahun** *tah-hoon*
Happy New Year!	**Selamat Tahun Baharu!** *Ser-lah-mat Tah-hoon Bah-har-roo!*
Happy Birthday!	**Selamat Hari Jadi!** *Ser-lah-mat Hah-ri Jah-dee!*

Months

January	**Januari** *Jah-noo-ah-ri*
February	**Februari** *Fer-broo-ah-ri*
March	**Mac** *Mahch*
April	**April** *Ah-pril*
May	**Mei** *Mey*
June	**Jun** *Joon*

July	**Julai** *Joo-lai*
August	**Ogos** *O-gos*
September	**September** *Seyp-teym-ber*
October	**Oktober** *Ok-to-ber*
November	**November** *No-veym-ber*
December	**Disember** *Di-seym-ber*

Seasons

spring	**bunga** *boo-ngah*
summer	**panas** *pah-nahs*
autumn	**luruh** *loo-rooh*
winter	**sejuk** *ser-jook*

There are two types of holidays in Malaysia, National holidays (observed nationwide) and State holidays. Traditional holidays for the various ethnic groups, such as the **Chinese New Year**, **Hari Raya** and **Deepavali**, follow the respective calendars, such as the Chinese lunar calendar, Islamic calendar and Hindu calendar. And therefore, their dates vary annually. Malaysians usually celebrate all the major festivals, irrespective of race.

Holidays

New Year's Day (Jan 1)
Chinese New Year (based on the Chinese Lunar calendar, the first day of the first Lunar month)
Awal Muharram (also known as **Maal Hijrah**, based on the Islamic calendar)
Prophet Muhammad's Birthday (also known as **Maulidur Rasul**, based on the Islamic calendar)

Labour Day (May 1)
Wesak Day (based on the Chinese Lunar calendar)
Agong's (King's) Birthday (based on the birthday of the current King/ruler)
National Day (Aug 31) (also known as **Merdeka Day**)
Deepavali (based on the Hindu calendar)
Hari Raya Puasa (also known as **Eid-ul-Fitri**, based on the Islamic calendar)
Christmas Day (Dec 25)
Hari Raya Haji (also known as **Eid-ul-Adha**, Muslims will usually make their pilgrimage to Mecca at this time)

Conversion Tables

When you know	Multiply by	To find
When you know	Multiply by	To find
ounces	28.3	grams
pounds	0.45	kilograms
inches	2.54	centimeters
feet	0.3	meters
miles	1.61	kilometers
square inches	6.45	sq. **centimeters**
square feet	0.09	sq. meters
square miles	2.59	sq. kilometers
pints (U.S./Brit)	0.47/0.56	liters
gallons (U.S./Brit)	3.8/4.5 liters	
Fahrenheit	5/9, after 32	Centigrade
Centigrade	9/5, then +32	Fahrenheit

Kilometers to Miles Conversions

1 km = 0.62 miles	**50 km** = 31 miles
5 km = 3.1 miles	**100 km** = 62 miles
10 km = 6.2 miles	

Measurement

1 gram	= **1000 milligrams**	= 0.035 oz.
1 kilogram (kg)	= **1000 grams**	= 2.2 lb
1 liter (l)	= **1000 milliliters**	= 1.06 U.S./0.88
1 centimeter	= **10 millimeters**	= 0.4 inch (cm)
1 meter (m)	= **100 centimeters**	= 39.37 inches/3.28 ft.
1 kilometer	= **1000 meters**	= 0.62 mile (km)

Temperature

-40°C = -40°F	**-1°C** = 30°F	**20°C** = 68°F
-30°C = -22°F	**0°C** = 32°F	**25°C** = 77°F
-20°C = -4°F	**5°C** = 41°F	**30°C** = 86°F
-10°C = 14°F	**10°C** = 50°F	**35°C** = 95°F
-5°C = 23°F	**15°C** = 59°F	

Oven Temperature

100° C = 212° F	**177° C** = 350° F
121° C = 250° F	**204° C** = 400° F
149° C = 300° F	**260° C** = 500° F

Dictionary

kerajang aluminium aluminum foil

...eramat Malay shrine

...rang-kerangan shellfish

...eta car

...ta api bawah tanah subway

...a sewa rental car

...sorong bayi stroller

...train

...ng throat

...g brooch

...aper towel

...hild's seat

...elchair

...tak highchair

...side effect

...an decision

...kenegara cou...

...d pakaian dres...

...da cola

...lam pond

...lam renang swim...

...lam renang luar o...

...lam renang dalama...

...lar collar

...omputer computer

...ondom condom

...onsert concert

...opi coffee

...osong empty

...ot coat

...ota fort

...otak box

...otor dirty

...rim cream; ointment

...rim cukur sh...

...rystal s...

A

a.m. *pagi*
accept v *menerima*
access *masuk*
accident *kemalangan*
accommodation *penginapan*
account n *akaun*
adapter *adaptor*
address n *alamat*
admission (fees) *bayaran masuk*
after *selepas*
afternoon *tengah hari*
aftershave *losen selepas bercukur*
again *semula; lagi*
age *umur*
agency *agensi*
AIDS *AIDS*
air *udara*
air conditioning *alat hawa dingin;penyaman udara*
airline *sistem penerbangan*
airmail *mel udara*
airplane *kapal terbang*
airport *lapanpan terbang*
airport tax *cukai penerbangan*
aisle seat *tempat duduk tepi lorong*
aisle *lorong; ruang sayap*
alarm clock *jam loceng*
alcohol *alkohol; arak*
allergic reaction *reaksi alah*
allergic *alah; alergi*

allow v *membenarkan*
alone *sendirian*
alter v **(clothing)** *meminda (pakaian)*
alternate route *jalan yang lain*
aluminum foil *kerajang aluminium*
amazing *mengagumkan*
ambulance *ambulans*
American *orang Amerika*
amount *jumlah; amaun*
amusement park *taman hiburan*
anemic *penyakit anemia*
anesthesia n *ubat bius*
animal *haiwan*
ankle *buku lali; pergelangan kaki*
antibiotic *antibiotik*
antiques store *kedai antik*
antiseptic cream *krim antiseptik*
anyone *sesiapa*
anything *apa-apa*
apartment *pangsapuri; apartmen*
appendix (body part) *umbai usus*
appetizer *pembuka selera*
apple *epal*
appointment *janji temu*
apricot *aprikot*
arcade *arked*
area code *kod kawasan*
arm *tangan*
around (the corner) *di sebalik (selekoh)*
arrivals (airport) *ketibaan*
arrive v *tiba*

| adj | adjective | BE | British English | prep | preposition |
| adv | adverb | n | noun | v | verb |

artery *arteri*
arthritis *artritis*
artificial sweetener *pemanis tiruan*
Asian (restaurant) *restoran Asia*
asparagus *pucuk asparagus*
aspirin *aspirin*
assistance *pertolongan; bantuan*
asthma *penyakit lelah; asma*
ATM card *kad ATM*
attached (in a relationship) *sedang menjalin hubungan*
attack (on person) *serangan*
attend v *menghadiri*
attraction (place) *tempat menarik*
attractive *menarik*
audio *audio*
Australian *warga Australia*
authentic *asli*
automatic car *kereta automatik*

B

baby bottle *botol bayi*
baby food *makanan bayi*
baby wipe *tisu lembap untuk bayi*
baby *bayi*
babysitter *pengasuh bayi*
back (body part) *belakang*
backpack *beg galas*
bacon *bakon*
bag *beg*
baggage BE *bagasi*
baggage claim *tuntutan bagasi*
baggage ticket *tiket bagasi*
bake v *membakar*
bakery *kedai roti*
ballet *balet (tarian)*
banana *pisang*
bandage *pembalut*

bank *bank*
bar (place) *bar*
barbecue *barbeku*
barber *tukang gunting rambut*
baseball *besbol*
basket (grocery store) *bakul*
basketball *bola keranjang*
bathroom *bilik air*
batik *kain batik*
battery *bateri*
battleground *tempat pertempuran*
be v *menjadi*
beach *pantai*
bean curd *tauhu*
beautiful *cantik*
bed and breakfast *tempat penginapan dengan sarapan pagi*
bed *katil*
beef *daging lembu*
beer *bir*
before *sebelum*
begin v *bermula*
beginner (skill level) *orang yang baru belajar*
behind (direction) *belakang*
beige *kuning air*
belt *tali pinggang*
berth *tempat berlabuh*
best *terbaik*
bet v *bertaruh*
better *lebih baik*
beverage *minuman*
bicycle *basikal*
big *besar*
bigger *lebih besar*
bike route *jalan basikal*
bikini *bikini*

bill v (charge) *bil;*
  ~ n (money) *wang kertas*
bird *burung*
birthday *hari jadi*
bites n *gigitan*
black pepper *lada hitam*
black *hitam*
bladder *pundi kencing*
bland *tawar*
blanket *selimut*
bleed v *berdarah*
blood pressure *tekanan darah*
blood *darah*
blouse *blaus; baju wanita*
blow-dry (hair) *ditiup kering*
blue *biru*
board v *menaiki*
boarding pass *pas masuk*
boat *bot; sampan*
boil (cooking method) *rebus*
bone *tulang*
book n *buku;* v *menempah*
bookstore *kedai buku*
boots *kasut but*
boring *bosan*
botanical garden *taman botani*
bother v *ganggu, menggangu*
bottle opener *pembuka botol*
bottle *botol*
bowl *mangkuk*
box *kotak*
boxing match *pertandingan tinju*
boy *budak lelaki*
boyfriend *teman lelaki*
bra *coli*
bracelet *rantai tangan; gelang tangan*
brakes (car) *brek*

brave adj *berani*
bread *roti*
breaded (cooking method) *bersalut serbuk roti*
break v *pecah*
break down v *rosak*
breakfast *sarapan pagi*
break-in (burglary) *kejadian pecah rumah; rompakan*
breast *buah dada*
breastfeed *menyusu bayi dengan susu ibu*
breathe deeply *tarik nafas*
breathe v *bernafas*
bridge *jambatan*
briefs (clothing) *seluar dalam*
bring v *membawa*
British *orang British*
broccoli *brokoli*
broken (bone) *patah;* (machine) *rosak;* (glass) *pecah*
brooch *kerongsang*
broom *penyapu*
brother (older) *abang*
brother (younger) *adik*
brown *coklat; perang*
bug *pepijat*
building *bangunan*
burn v *membakar*
bus station *stesen bas*
bus stop *perhentian bas*
bus ticket *tiket bas*
bus tour *persiaran dengan bas*
bus *bas*
business *bisnes; perniagaan*
business center *pusat perniangaan*
business class *kelas perniagaan*

business hours *waktu perniagaan*
busy *sibuk*
butcher *penjual daging*
butter *mentega*
buttocks *punggung*
buy v *membeli*
bye *selamat jalan*

C

cabbage *kubis*
cabin *kabin*
cable *car kereta kabel*
café *kafe*
call v *panggil;* ~ n *panggilan telefon*
calories *kalori*
camera case *sarung kamera*
camera store *kedai kamera*
camera *kamera*
camp v *berkhemah*
camping stove *dapur khemah*
campsite *tapak perkhemahan*
can opener *pembuka tin*
can n *tin;* ~ *(yes) boleh*
Canadian *warga Kanada*
cancel v *membatalkan*
candy *gula-gula*
canned goods *makanan tin*
canyon *kanyon*
capsicum *lada benggala*
car hire [BE] *menyewa kereta*
car park [BE] *tempat meletak kereta*
car rental *sewa kereta*
car seat *tempat duduk kereta*
car *kereta*
carafe *serahi*
carambola [starfruit] *belimbing*
card *kad*
carp (fish) *ikan kap*

carrot *lobak merah*
carry-on *beg tangan*
cart *troli*
carton *karton*
carvings, n *ukiran*
cash n *wang tunai;* ~ v *tunaikan cek*
cash advance *wang pendahuluan*
cashier *juruwang*
casino *kasino*
castle *istana kota*
cathedral *gereja besar*
Catholic *Katolik*
cauliflower *kubis bunga*
cave *gua*
CD *CD*
celery *saderi*
cell phone *telefon mudah alih; telefon bimbit*
Celsius *Celsius*
centimeter *sentimeter*
ceramic spoon *sudu seramik*
cereal *bijian*
certificate *sijil*
chair lift (cable car) *lif kerusi*
chair *kerusi*
change v *menukar; tukar;* ~ n **(money)** *wang kecil*
charcoal *arang*
charge v **(credit card)** *membayar*
cheap *murah*
cheaper *lebih murah*
check v **(something)** *memeriksa (sesuata);* ~ n *cek*
check-in *mendaftar masuk*
check-out *mendaftar keluar*
checking account *akaun semasa*
cheese *keju*

chemical toilet *tandas kimia*
chemist [BE] *ahli kimia*
cheque [BE] *cek*
cherry *ceri*
chest (body part) *dada*
chest pain *sakit dada*
chewing gum *gula-gula getah*
chicken *ayam*
child *kanak-kanak; budak*
child's seat *kerusi budak*
children's portion *bahagian kanak-kanak*
China *negara Cina*
china *tembikar*
Chinese (person) *orang Cina*
chocolates *coklat*
chopsticks *penyepit*
church *gereja*
cigar *cerut*
cigarette *rokok*
city *hall dewan bandar raya*
clam *kepah*
class *kelas*
classical music *muzik klasik*
clay pot *belanga*
clean v *membersihkan;* ~ adj *bersih*
cleaning product *produk membersih*
cleaning supplies *bahan membersih*
clear v *batal*
cliff *cenuram*
clock *jam*
close v *tutup;* ~ adj *dekat*
closed *tertutup*
clothing store *kedai pakaian*
clothing *pakaian; baju*
club *kelab*
coat *kot*

cod (type of fish) *ikan kod*
coffee shop *kedai kopi*
coin *duit syiling*
cola *kola*
cold *dingin; sejuk*
cold (sickness) *selsema*
colleague *rakan sekerja*
collect call *panggilan pindah bayaran*
cologne *air kolong*
color *warna*
comb *sikat*
come v *datang*
company (firm) *syarikat*
complain *mengadu*
complaint *aduan*
computer *komputer*
concert hall *dewan konsert*
concert *konsert*
condition (medical) *keadaan (kesihatan)*
conditioner (hair) *perapi (rambut); kondisioner*
condom *kondom*
conference *persidangan*
confirm v *mengesahkan*
congestion *kesesakan*
connect v **(internet)** *menyambung*
connection (internet) *sambungan*
constipated *sembelit*
consulate *pejabat konsul; konsulat*
consultant *pakar runding*
contact v *berhubungan*
contact *lens kanta sentuh*
contact lens solution *cecair pencuci kanta sentuh*
contagious *berjangkit*
contain *mengandungi*

convention hall *dewan persidangan*
conversion table *jadual pertukaran*
conveyor belt *tali sawat penyampai*
cook v *memasak*
cooking gas *gas memasak*
cool (temperature) *dingin; agak sejuk*
copper *kuprum*
corkscrew *skru pencungkil gabus*
corn (vegetable) *jagung*
corner *selekoh*
cost *harga; kos*
costume jewelry *barang kemas kostum; hiasan*
cot *katil budak*
cotton *kapas*
cough *batuk*
counter n *kaunter*
country code *kod negara*
court (sports) *gelanggang*
cover charge *bayaran masuk*
crab (animal) *ketam*
cramps (menstruation) *kejang datang haid*
crash v (car) *kemalangan*
cream/ointment *krim; krim salap*
credit card *kad kredit*
crew neck *kolar berbentuk bulat*
crib *katil bayi*
crystal *krystal*
cup *cawan*
cured meat *daging awet*
currency exchange office *pejabat pertukaran wang asing*
currency exchange *pertukaran wang asing*
currency *mata wang*
current account [BE] *akaun semasa*

customs *kastam*
cut v (hair) *menggunting;* ~ n (injury) *luka*
cute *comel*
cycling *mengayuh basikalcigar*

D

dairy *hasil tenusu*
damage v *merosakkan,* n *kerosakan*
damaged *telah rosak*
dance club *kelab menari*
dance v *menari*
dancing *sedang menari*
danger *bahaya*
dark *gelap*
date (calendar) *tarikh*
dates (fruit) *kurma*
day *hari*
deaf *pekak*
debit card *kad debit*
decision *keputusan*
deck chair *kerusi dek*
declare v *mengisytiharkan; mendeklarasi*
decline v (credit card) *menolak*
deeply *jauh ke dalam*
degrees (temperature) *darjah*
delay v *menangguh;* n *penangguhan; kelewatan*
delete v *memadam*
delicatessen *delikatesen*
delicious *sedap*
denim *kain demin*
dentist *doktor gigi*
denture *gigi palsu*
deodorant *penyahbau*
department store *kedai serbaneka*
departure *perlepasan*

deposit v memasukkan; ~ n (bank) menabung
detergent bahan cuci
diabetes penyakit kencing manis
dial v mendail
diamond berlian
diaper kain lampin
diarrhea cirit-birit
diesel minyak diesel
difficult susah
digital photo gambar digital
digital print cetakan gambar digital
dining room ruang makan
dinner makan malam
direction arah
dirty kotor
disabled accessible [BE] mesra kurang upaya
disabled kurang upaya; cacat
disconnect (computer) memberhentikan sambungan
discount diskaun
dish (kitchen) pinggan mangkuk
dishes (food) lauk-pauk
dishwasher mesin basuh pinggan mangkuk
dishwashing liquid cecair pencuci pinggan mangkuk
display case kotak pameran
display v mempamerkan; n pameran
disposable razor pencukur pakai buang
disposable pakai buang
dive v menyelam
diving equipment kelengkapan menyelam
divorce v bercerai; n perceraian
dizzy pening

do not disturb janggan ganggu; **janggang** kacau
doctor doktor
dog anjing
doll patung
dollar (U.S.) dolar
domestic flight penerbangan domestik
domestic domestik
door pintu
dormitory asrama
double bed katil kelamin
downtown pusat bandar
dozen dozen
draw lukis; melukis
drawer laci
dress (piece of clothing) baju
dress code kod pakaian
drink menu menu minuman
drink v minum; ~ n minuman
drinking water air minuman
drive v memandu
driver's license number nombor lesen memandu
drop (medicine) titik
drowsiness kepeningan
dry cleaner kedai mencuci kering
duck (animal) itik
during semasa
duty (tax) cukai; duti
duty-free bebas cukai
DVD DVD

E

ear telinga
earache sakit telinga
early awal
earrings anting-anting
east timur

easy *senang*
eat v *makan*
economy class *kelas ekonomi*
egg *telur*
eggplant [aubergine] *terung ungu*
elbow *siku*
electric outlet *saluran elektrik*
elevator *tangga gerak*
e-mail address *alamat e-mel*
e-mail *e-mel*
emergency exit *pintu keluar kecemasan*
emergency *kecemasan*
empty *kosong;* v *mengosongkan*
end v *tamat*
engaged (in a relationship) *bertunang*
English *Inggeris*
engrave v *mengukir*
enjoy v *menikmati*
enter v *masuk*
entertainment *hiburan*
entrance *pintu masuk*
envelope *sampul surat*
epilepsy *epilepsi*
equipment *kelengkapan; perkakasan*
escalator *tangga gerak; eskalator*
e-ticket *tiket elektronik*
evening *petang*
excess *lebihan*
exchange rate *kadar pertukaran wang asing*
exchange v *menukar*
excursion *rombongan*
excuse me v *maafkan saya*
excuse n *alasan*
exhausted *amat letih; keletihan*
exit v *keluar;* ~ n *pintu keluar*
expensive *mahal*

expert (skill level) *pakar*
expiration date *tarikh lupus*
express *ekspres*
extension (phone) *sambungan*
external *use*
extra large (size) *(saiz) tambah*
extra small (size) *(saiz) lebih kecil*
extra *tambahan*
extract v **(tooth)** *mencabut*
eye *mata*

F

fabric *kain*
face *muka*
facial *rawatan muka*
facility *kemudahan*
family *keluarga*
fan (appliance) *kipas*
far *jauh*
fare (e.g taxi fare) *tambang*
farm *ladang; kebun*
far-sighted (eye condition) *rabun dekat*
fast food *makanan segara*
fast *cepat*
faster *lebih cepat*
fat free *bebas lemak*
father *ayah; bapa*
fax number *nombor faks*
fax v *menghantar faks;* ~ n *faks*
fee *bayaran*
feed v *menyuap*
ferry *feri*
fever *deman*
field (sports) *padang*
fill out v **(form)** *mengisi*
fill up v **(food)** *menambah*
filling (tooth) *tampalan*

film (camera) *filem*
fine (fee) *denda*
fine (greetings) *khabar baik*
finger *jari*
fingernail *kuku jari*
fire *api*
fire department *jabatan api dan bomba*
fire door *pintu penghadang api*
first *pertama*
first class *kelas pertama*
fit (clothing) *muat*
fitting room *bilik mencuba pakaian*
fix v **(repair)** *membaiki*
fixed-price menu *menu dengan harga tetap*
flashlight *lampu suluh*
flats (shoes) *kasut tidak bertumit*
flight *penerbangan*
floor *lantai*
florist *penjual bunga*
flower *bunga*
fly v *terbang; menerbang*
fly (insect) *lalat*
folk music *muzik rakyat*
food *makanan*
foot *kaki*
football game [BE] *perlawanan bola sepak*
for *untuk*
forecast *ramalan*
forest *hutan*
fork *garpu*
form (fill-in) *borang*
formula (baby) *susu bayi*
fountain *pancuran air*
free *bebas*
freezer *penyejuk beku*

fresh *segar*
fried (cooking method) *goreng*
friend *kawan; rakan*
fruits *buah-buahan*
frying *pan kuali leper*
full *penuh*
full-service *perkhidmatan penuh*
fun *berseronok*
funny *lucu*

G

game *permainan*
garage *garaj*
garbage bag *beg sampah*
garlic *bawang putih*
gas station *stesen minyak*
gas *minyak*
gate (airport) *pintu*
gay (happy) *meriah; riang*
gel (hair) *gel*
get off (a train/bus/subway) *turun*
get to *pergi ke*
gift *hadiah*
gin *gin*
girl *gadis; anak perempuan*
girlfriend *teman wanita*
give v *memberi*
glass (drinking) *gelas*
glass (material) *kaca*
glasses (spectacles) *cermin mata*
gluten *gluten*
go v **(somewhere)** *pergi*
gold *emas*
golf course *padang golf*
golf tournament *pertandingan golf*
good *baik; bagus*
good afternoon *selamat tengah hari*
good evening *selamat petang*

good morning selamat pagi
goodbye selamat jalan
goods barangan
grandchild cucu
grandchildren cucu-cicit
grandfather datuk
grandmother nenek
grape anggur
grapefruit limau gedang
grater pemarut
gray kelabu
green hijau
grocery store kedai runcit
ground floor tingkat bawah
group kumpulan
guide (tourist) n pemandu
  (pelancong)
guide book buku panduan
guide dog anjing pemandu
gym gim
gynecologist doktor pakar puan

H

hair dryer alat pengering rambut
hair salon salum rambut
hair rambut
hairbrush berus rambut
haircut potongan rambut
hairspray penyembur rambut
hairstyle gaya rambut
hairstylist pendandan rambut
halal halal
half hour setengah jam
half setengah
half-kilo setengah kilo
hall dewan
ham (food) ham
hammer tukul

hand luggage [BE] bagasi tangan
hand tangan
handbag [BE] beg tangan
handicapped kurang upaya; cacat
handicapped-accessible mesra kurang
  upaya
hangover pening kerana terlalu
happy gembira
hat topi
have v mendapatkan
hawker centre pusat makanan
hay fever deman alergi
head (body part) kepala
headache sakit kepala
headphones fonkepala
health food store kedai makanan sihat
health kesihatan
hearing impaired cacat pendengaran
heart condition sakit jantung
heart jantung
heat haba
heater pemanas
heating [BE] memanas
height ketinggian
hello helo
helmet topi keledar
help pertolongan; bantuan
here sini I
hi hai
high tinggi
highchair kerusi tinggi budak
high-heels kasut bertumit tinggi
highlights (hair) penyerlah
highway lebuhraya
hill bukit
hire v [BE] menyewa
hired car [BE] kereta sewa

hitchhike v *mengembara tumpang*
hockey *hoki*
hold v *pegang*
holiday [BE] *percutian*
home *rumah*
hospital *hospital*
hostel *asrama*
hot (temperature) *panas*; ~ **(spicy)** *pedas*
hot water *air panas*
hotel *hotel; rumah penginapan*
hour *jam*
house *rumah*
household goods *barangan rumah*
housekeeping services *perkhidmatan mengemas bilik*
how are you *apa khabar*
how much (price) *berapa*
how *bagaimana*
hug v *memeluk*
hungry *lapar*
hurt *sakit*
husband *suami*

I

I *aku, saya*
ibuprofen *ibuprofen* (see **painkiller**)
ice *ais*
icy *berais; sangut sejuk*
identification (card) *(kad) pengenalan*
ill *sakit*
immigration *imigrasi*
in *dalam*
include v *termasuk*
indoor *dalam rumah*
indoor pool *kolam renang dalaman*
inexpensive *murah*

infected *terjangkit*
infection *jangkitan*
information *maklumat*
information desk *kaunter keterangan*
insect bite *gigitan serangga*
insect repellent *penghalau serangga*
insert v **(on an ATM)** *memasukkan*
inside *dalam*
insomnia *insomnia*
instant message *mesej segera*
insulin *insulin*
insurance *insurans*
insurance company *syarikat insurans*
interested *minat; tertarik*
interesting *menarik*
international *antarabangsa*
international flight *penerbangan antarabangsa*
international student card *kad pelajar antarabangsa*
internet cafe *kafe internet*
internet service *perkhidmatan internet*
internet *internet*
interpreter *penterjemahan*
intersection *persimpangan*
into *ke dalam*
introduce v *memperkenalkan*
invoice *invois*
Irish *orang Ireland*
iron (clothes) v *menyeterika*; ~ n *besi*
itemize *butiran*

J

jacket *jaket*
jackfruit *buah nangka*
jade *jed*
jam (food) *jem*
jam (traffic) n *kesesakan*; v *sesak*

jar *balang*
jaw *rahang*
jazz club *kelab muzik jaz*
jazz *muzik jaz*
jeans *seluar jean*
jelly (food) *agar-agar*
jeweler *kedai emas*
jewelry *barang kemas*
join v *menyertai*
joint (body part) *sendi*
joke *bergurau; bersenda*
juice *jus*

K

keep *simpan*
keep refrigerated *simpan sejuk*
key *kunci;* ~ *card kad kunci*
key ring *cecincin kunci*
kick *tendang*
kiddie pool *kolam renang budak*
kidney (body part) *buah pinggang*
kilogram *kilogram*
kilometer *kilometer*
kind (person) *baik hati*
kiss v *mencium*
kitchen *dapur*
kiwi fruit *buah kiwi*
knee *lutut*
knife *pisau*
know *tahu*
knowledge *pengetahuan*

L

lactose intolerant *penyakit kurang upaya memproses laktosa*
lady *wanita; perempuan*
lake *tasik*
lamb (meat) *kambing*
lamp *lampu*

language *bahasa*
large *besar*
last *terakhir*
last night *malam tadi; semalam*
last week *minggu yang lalu*
late (time) *lewat*
later *nanti*
laundromat *kedai dobi layan diri*
laundry *kain kotor*
laundry facility *kemudahan tempat mendobi*
laundry service *perkhidmatan mendobi*
lawyer *peguam*
lazy *malas*
leaded (fuel) *(minyak) berplumbum*
leaf *daun*
learn, v *belajar*
leather *kulit*
leave (depart) v *berlepas* **(planes)**; *bertolak* **(buses, trains, etc.)**
left (direction) *kiri*
leg *kaki*
lemon *lemon*
lemonade *air lemon*
lemongrass *serai*
lens *kanta*
less *kurang*
lesson (learnt a lesson) *pengajaran*
letter *surat*
lettuce *selada*
library *perpustakaan*
licence *lesen*
life boat *bot keselamatan*
life jacket *jaket keselamatan*
lifeguard *anggota penyelamat*
lift *lif*
light n *lampu;* ~ v **(cigarette)** *menyalakan*

light adj (bright) *terang;* adj (not heavy) *ringan*
lightbulb *mentol*
lighter *pemetik api*
like v *suka*
lime *limau nipis*
line *garis; barisan*
lip *bibir*
liquor store *kedai arak*
liter *liter*
little *sedikit*
live v *tinggal*
liver (body part) *hati*
loafers *kasut lepak*
lobster *udang galah*
local *tempatan*
lock n *mangga*
lock up *mengunci*
locker *gerobok; lokar*
log off *log keluar*
log on *log masuk*
long sleeves *lengan panjang*
long *panjang*
long-sighted [BE] *rabun dekat*
look v *melihat; tengok*
lose v (something) *hilang*
lost and found *hilang dan terjumpa*
lost *sesat*
lotion *losen*
loud *bising*
love *cinta*
low *rendah*
luggage *bagasi*
luggage cart *troli bagasi*
luggage locker *lokar bagasi*
lunch *makan tengah hari*
lung *paru-paru*

M

magazine *majalah*
Madam/Mrs *Puan*
magnificent *menakjubkan*
mail v *menghantar surat;* ~ n *surat*
mailbox *peti surat*
main attraction *tempat tarikan utama*
main course *hidangan utama*
make up (face) v *bersolek*
Malay *Melayu*
mall *pasar raya*
man *lelaki*
manager *pengurus*
mango *buah mangga*
manicure *rias tangan dan kuku*
manual car *kereta manual*
map n *peta*
market *pasar*
married *telah berkahwin*
marry v *mengahwini*
mass (church service) *Misa*
massage *pengurutan*
mat (rug) *tikar*
match n *mancis*
meal *hidangan*
measure v (someone) *mengukur*
measuring cup *cawan ukuran*
measuring spoon *sudu ukuran*
mechanic *mekanik*
medicine *ubat*
medium (size) *sederhana*
meet v (someone) *bertemu*
meeting room *bilik mesyuarat*
meeting *mesyuarat*
membership card *kad keahlian*
memorial (place) *tugu peringatan*
memory card *kad memori*

mend v *membaiki*
men's *lelaki*
menstrual cramp *sakit perut akibat haid*
menstruation *datang bulan; haid*
menu *menu*
message *pesanan*
meter (parking) *meter*
microwave *ketuhar gelombang mikro*
midday [BE] *tengah hari*
midnight *tengah malam*
mileage *perbatuan*
milk *susu*
mini-bar *bar mini*
minute *minit*
Miss *Cik*
missing (something) *hilang;*
  (someone) *rindu*
mistake *kesilapan*
mobile phone [BE] *telefon mudah alih;*
  telefon bimbit
mobility *pergerakan*
money *duit; wang*
monorail *monorel*
month *bulan*
mop *mop*
more *lebih*
morning *pagi*
mosque *masjid*
mother *ibu; emak*
motion sickness *mabuk gerakan*
motor boat *motorbot*
motorcycle *motorsikal*
motorway (highway) [BE] *lebuhraya*
mountain *gunung*
mousse (hair) *mousse*
mouth *mulut*
movie theater *panggung wayang*

movie *wayang*
Mr/Sir *Encik*
Mrs/Madam *Puan*
mug v *merompak*
multiple-trip (ticket)
  (tiket) pelbagai perjalanan
muscle *otot*
museum *muzium*
mushroom *cendawan*
music *store kedai muzik*
music *muzik*

N

nail *kuku*
name *nama*
napkin *napkin*
nappy [BE] *kain lampin*
nationality *kewarganegaraan*
nature *preserve kawasan hutan simpan*
nauseous *rasa mual*
near *dekat; nearby berdekatan*
near-sighted *berpandangan dekat*
neck *leher; ~lace rantai leher*
need v *memerlukan*
new *baru*
newspaper *surat khabar*
newsstand *gerai surat khabar*
next to *sebelah*
next *seterusnya*
nice *baik*
night *malam*
nightclub *kelab malam*
no *tidak; bukan*
non-alcoholic *tanpa alkohol*
non-smoking *dilarang merokok*
noodles *mee*
noon *tengah hari*
north *utara*

nose *hidung*
notes [BE] *nota*
nothing *tiada apa-apa*
notify v *menghubungi*
novice (skill level) *baru belajar*
now *sekarang*
number *nombor*
nurse *jururawat*
nuts (food) *kacang*

O

office *pejabat*
oatmeal *bubur oat*
octopus *sotong kurita*
office hours *waktu pejabat*
oil *minyak*
OK *OK*
old (person) *tua;* **(long ago)** *lama*
old town *bandar lama*
olive *buah zaitun*
on the corner *di selekoh*
once *sekali*
one *satu*
one-way (ticket) *sehala*
one-way street *jalan sehala*
only *hanya*
on-time *tepat masa*
open *buka*
opera *opera*
opposite *bertentangan*
optician *pakar optik*
orange (color) *oren*
orchestra *orkestra*
order v *memesan*
outdoor pool *kolam renang luar*
outside *di luar*
over the counter (medication) *dijual di kaunter*

overdone *melampau*
overnight *bermalam*
ox *lembu jantan*
oxtail *ekor lembu*
oyster *tiram*

P

p.m. *petang*
pacifier *puting*
pack v *mengemas*
package *bungkusan*
pad (for menstruation) [BE] *tuala wanita*
paddling pool [BE] *kolam renang kanak-kanak*
pages (in a book) *muka surat*
pain *sakit*
painkiller *ubat tahan sakit*
pajamas *baju tidur*
palace *istana*
pants *seluar panjang*
pantyhose *sarung kaki wanita*
papaya (fruit) *betik*
paper towel *kertas tisu*
paper *kertas*
paracetamol [BE] *panadol* (see painkiller)
park v *meletak kereta;* ~ n *taman*
parking *lot tempat meletak kereta*
parking meter *meter meletak kereta*
part-time *sambilan*
passenger *penumpang*
passport control *kastam dan imigresen*
passport *pasport*
password *kata laluan*
pastry shop *kedai pastri*
path *lorong; laluan kecil*
pay phone *telefon awam*
pay v *membayar*

pea *kacang pis*
peach *pic*
peak (of a mountain) *puncak*
pear *pir*
pearl *mutiara*
pedestrian *pejalan kaki*
pediatrician *doktor pakar kanak-kanak*
pedicure *rawatan kaki*
peeled (cooking method) *tanpa kulit*
pen *pen*
penicillin *penisilin*
penis *zakar*
pepper *lada*
per *se-;* **~hour** *sejam;* **~day** *sehar;*
  ~night *semalam;* **~week** *seminggu*
perfume *minyak wangi*
period (menstrual) *datang bulan; haid*
period (of time) *jangka masa*
permit v *membenarkan*
personal identification number (PIN)
  nombor pengenalan diri
petite *kecil molek*
petrol [BE] *petrol*
petrol station [BE] *stesen petrol*
pewter *piuter*
pharmacy *farmasi*
phone v *menelefon;* ~ n *telefon*
phone call *panggilan telefon*
phone card *kad telefon*
phone number *nombor telefon*
photo *gambar*
photocopy *fotokopi*
photography *fotografi*
pick up (something) *mengutip*
picnic area *kawasan berkelah*
piece *keping*
pill (birth control) *pil pencegah hamil*

pillow *bantal*
pineapple *nanas*
pink *merah jambu*
pizzeria *kedai pizza*
place n *tempat*
plan *rancangan; pelan*
plane *kapal terbang*
plastic *plastik*
plastic wrap *pembalut plastik*
plate *pinggan*
platform *pelantar*
platinum *platinum*
play v *bermain;* ~ n **(theatre)** *sandiwara*
playground *taman permainan*
playpen *kandang main*
please *sila*
pleased *gembira*
plum *buah plum*
plunger *pelocok*
plus size *saiz tambah*
poach (cooking method) *reneh*
pocket *poket*
poison *racun*
police *polis*
police report *laporan polis*
police station *balai polis*
pomegranate *buah delima*
pomelo *limau bali*
pond *kolam*
pool *kolam renang*
pop music *muzik pop*
porcelain *porselin*
pork *daging babi*
porridge *bubur*
portion *bahagian*
post [BE] *pos*
post office *pejabat pos*

postbox [BE] *peti surat*
postcard *poskad*
pot *periuk*
potato *kentang*
pottery (goods) *tembikar*
poultry *ayam*
pregnant *hamil*
prescribe v *mempreskripsikan*
prescription *preskripsi*
press v **(clothing)** *menyeterika*
price *harga*
print v *mencetak*
problem *masalah*
prohibit v *melarang*
pronounce v *menyebut*
Protestant *Protestan*
public *awam*
pull v *menarik*
purple *ungu*
purpose *tujuan*
purse *dompet wanita*
push v *menolak*
pushchair [BE] *kerusi sorong bayi*

Q

quality *kualiti*
queen *ratu*
question *soalan*
queue *barisan*
quick *cepat*
quiet *sunyi; senyap*

R

rabbit *arnab*
radio *radio*
radish *lobak putih*
railway station [BE] *stesen kereta api*
rain n *hujan*
raincoat *baju hujan*

rainforest *hutan hujan*
ramp *tanjakan*
rap (music) *muzik rap*
rape *rogol*
rare (object) *jarang*
rash n *ruam*
rate (exchange rate) *kadar*
rat *tikus*
ravine *gaung*
raw *mentah*
reach v *tiba*
read *baca; membaca*
ready *sedia*
real *benar; tulen*
really *sangat; sungguh*
reason *alasan; sebab*
receipt *resit*
receive v *menerima*
recharge v *mengecas semula*
recommend v *mencadangkan; mengesyorkan*
recommendation *cadangan*
recycling *kitar semula*
red *merah*
refrigerator *peti sejuk*
refund *bayaran balik*
region *rantau*
registered mail *surat berdaftar*
regular (normal) *biasa*
relationship *hubungan*
rent v *menyewa*
rental car *kereta sewa*
repair v *memperbaiki*
repeat v *mengulangi*
reservation desk *kaunter tempahan*
reservation *tempahan*

reserve v *menempah*
resort (holiday) *tempat peranginan*
restaurant *restoran*
restroom (formal/informal) *bilik air/
tandas*
retired *bersara*
return (something) v *mengembalikan;*
~ **(return ticket)** n [BE] *ulang-alik*
reverse v **(the charges)** [BE] *(caj)
balikan*
rib (body part) *tulang rusuk*
rice *nasi*
right (direction) *kanan*
right of way *hak lalu-lalang*
ring *cincin*
river *sungai*
road *jalan*
road map *peta jalan*
roast v *memanggang*
rob v *merompak*
robbed *dirompak*
romantic *romantis*
room *bilik*
room (double) *bilik kelamin*
room (single) *bilik bujang*
room key *kunci bilik*
room service *servis bilik*
round-trip *ulang-alik*
rotten *busuk*
rubbish [BE] *sampah*
rubbish bag [BE] *beg sampah*
ruins *puing*
run *lari; melari*
rush (in a rush) *kesuntukan masa*

S

signature *tandatangan*
sad *sedih*

safe (object) *peti keselamatan;*
~ **(protected)** *selamat*
sales tax *cukai jualan*
salmon *ikan salmon*
salon *salun*
salty *masin*
sandals *kasut sandal*
sanitary napkin *tuala wanita*
sauce *sos*
saucepan *periuk*
sauna *mandi sauna*
sausage *sosej*
sauteed (cooking method) *masak
secara saute*
save v *simpan*
savings (account) *akaun simpanan*
scallion [spring onion] *daun bawang*
scanner *pengimbas*
schedule n *jadual waktu (perjalanan)*
school *sekolah*
science *sains*
scissors *gunting*
sea *laut*
seafood *makanan laut*
seat *tempat duduk*
seaweed *rumpai laut*
security *keselamatan*
see v *melihat*
self-service *layan diri*
sell v *menjual*
send v *menghantar*
senior citizen *orang tua*
separated (marriage) *berpisah*
service (in a restaurant) *perkhidmatan*
sexually transmitted disease *penyakit
kelamin*
shampoo *syampu*

sharp *tajam*
shaving cream *krim cukur*
sheet *kain cadar*
shellfish *kerang-kerangan*
ship v (mail) *menghantar dengan kapal*
shirt *kemeja*
shoe store *kedai kasut*
shoes *kasut*
shop *kedai*
shopping v *membeli-belah*
shopping area *kawasan membeli-belah*
shopping centre [BE] *pusat membeli-belah*
shopping mall *pasar raya*
short sleeves *lengan pendek*
short adj *pendek*
shorts *seluar pendek*
short-sighted [BE] *rabun jauh*
shoulder *bahu*
show v *menunjukkan*
shower (to wash) *mandi hujan*
shrimp *udang*
sick *sakit*
side dish *hidangan sampingan*
side effect *kesan sampingan*
sightseeing tour *lawatan*
sightseeing *melawat tempat-tempat*
silk *sutera*
silver *perak*
single (unmarried) *bujang*
single bed *katil bujang*
single room *bilik bujang*
sink *sink*
Sir/Mr *Encik*
sister (elder) *kakak;* **(younger)** *adik*
sit v *duduk*
size *saiz*

skin *kulit*
skirt *skirt*
sleep v *tidur*
sleeping bag *beg tidur*
slice (of something) *hirisan*
slippers *selipar*
slower *lebih perlahan*
slowly *perlahan-lahan*
small *kecil*
smaller *lebih kecil*
smoke v *merokok*
smoking area *kawasan merokok*
snack bar *bar snek*
snacks *snek*
sneaker *kasut sukan*
snorkeling equipment *kelengkapan snorkel*
snow n *salji*
soap *sabun*
soccer *bola sepak*
sock *sarung kaki*
soda *air soda*
some *sedikit*
soother [BE] *puting untuk bayi*
sore throat *sakit kerongkong*
sorry *minta maaf*
soup *sup*
sour *masam*
south *selatan*
souvenir store *kedai cenderahati*
souvenir *cenderahati*
soy bean *kacang soya*
soymilk *susu soya*
spa *spa*
spare ribs *tulang rusuk*
sparkling water *air bergas*
speak v *bercakap*

special *istimewa; khusus*
specialist (doctor) *(doktor) pakar*
specimen *spesimen*
speeding *memandu melebihi had laju*
spell v *mengeja*
spicy *pedas*
spinach *bayam*
spine (body part) *tulang belakang*
spoon *sudu*
sporting goods *barangan sukan*
sports massage *pengurutan sukan*
sports *sukan*
sprain *terseliuh (v)*
squid *sotong*
stadium *stadium*
stairs *tangga*
stamp v **(a ticket)** *mengecap;* ~ n **(postage)** *stem*
start v *bermula*
starter [BE] *pembuka selera*
station *stesen*
statue *tugu*
stay v *menginap*
steak *stik*
steal v *mencuri*
steam n *wap air*
steamed (cooking method) *dikukus*
steamer *pengukus*
steep *curam*
sterling silver *perak tulen*
sting n *sengat*
stolen *telah dicuri*
stomach *perut*
stomachache *sakit perut*
stop v *berhenti*
store directory *papan panduan kedai*
storey [BE] *tingkat*

stove *dapur*
straight ahead *terus ke hadapan*
straight *lurus*
strange *pelik*
strawberry *strawberi*
stream (school) *jurusan*
stream *anak sungai*
stroller *kereta sorong bayi*
student *pelajar*
study v *belajar*
stunning *menakjubkan*
style (hair) *gaya*
subtitle *sari kata*
subway station *stesen kereta api bawah tanah*
subway *kereta api bawah tanah*
sugar *gula*
suit *sut*
suitcase *beg pakaian*
sun *matahari*
sunblock *losen pelindung matahari*
sunburn *selaran matahari*
sunglasses *cermin mata hitam*
sunny *cerah*
sunstroke *strok matahari*
supermarket *pasar raya*
supervision *penyeliaan; pengawasan*
surfboard *papan luncur air*
swallow v *menelan*
sweater *baju panas*
sweet (taste) *manis*
sweets [BE] *gula-gula*
swelling *bengkak*
swim v *berenang;* ~ **suit** *baju renang*
swordfish *ikan todak*
symbol (keyboard) *simbol*
syrup *sirap*

T

table *meja*
tablet (medicine) *pil (ubat)*
take (something) v *mengambil*
take away (food) [BE] *bungkus (makanan)*
take off v (clothes) *tanggal*
tampon *tampon*
taste v *rasa*
taxi *teksi*
tea *teh*
team *pasukan*
teaspoon *sudu the*
telephone *telefon*
temperature *suhu*
temple (religious) *kuil; tokong*
temporary *sementara*
tennis *tenis*
tent *khemah; ~ peg pasak khemah; ~ pole tiang khemah*
terminal (airport) *terminal (lapangan terbang)*
terrible *teruk*
text v (send a message) *menghantar teks*
thank v *berterima kasih*
thank you *terima kasih*
that *itu*
theater *panggung wayang; teater*
theft *kecurian*
there *sana*
thief *pencuri*
thigh *paha*
thirsty *dahaga*
this *ini*
thrash [rubbish] *sampah*
throat *kerongkong*

thunderstorm *ribut petir*
ticket *tiket; ~ office pejabat tiket*
tie (clothing) *tali leher*
tight adj *ketat*
tights [BE] *seluar sama sendat*
time *masa; ~table [BE] jadual waktu*
tire *tayar*
tired *letih*
tissue *tisu*
to go *pergi ke*
toasted bread *roti bakar*
tobacconist *penjual barang-barang tembakau*
today *hari ini*
toe *jari kaki; ~nail kuku kaki*
toilet [BE] *tandas*
toilet paper *tisu tandas*
tomorrow *esok*
tongue *lidah*
tonight *malam ini*
too *juga*
tooth *gigi; ~paste ubat gigi*
top up card (phone value) *kad tambah nilai*
total (amount) *jumlah*
tough (food) *liat*
tour *melancong; lawatan*
tourist information office *pejabat maklumat pelancong*
tourist *pelancong*
tow truck *trak penarik*
towel *tuala*
tower *menara*
town *bandar; ~ hall dewan bandar*
town square *pusat pekan*
toy *mainan*
traces *sisa-sisa*

track (train) *landasan*
traditional *tradisional*
traffic light *lampu isyarat*
trail *denai*
train *keretapi*
transfer v **(trains/flights)** *menukar*
translate v *menterjemah*
trash *sampah*
travel agency *agensi perlancong*
travel sickness *mabuk kembara*
traveler's check *cek kembara*
treat (to a drink) *belanja*
tree *pokok*
trim (hair cut) *memepat*
trip *perjalanan*
trolley [BE] *troli*
trousers [BE] *seluar panjang*
T-shirt *baju kemeja-T*
turn off (lights) *padamkan*
turn on (lights) *pasangkan*
TV *televisyen*
type v *menaip*
tyre [BE] *tayar*

U

ugly *hodoh*
umbrella *payung*
unattended *tanpa diawasi*
unconscious *tidak sedarkan diri*
underground [BE] *bawah tanah*
underground station [BE] *stensen bawah tanah*
underpants [BE] *seluar dalam*
understand v *faham*
underwear *pakaian dalam*
unemployed *penganggur*
United Kingdom *United Kingdom (U.K.)*
United States *(U.S.) Amerika Syarikat*

university *universiti*
unleaded (gas) *minyak tanpa plumbum*
unlimited *tanpa had*
upper *bahagian atas*
upset stomach *sakit perut*
urgent *penting*
urine *air kencing*
use v *menggunakan*

V

vacancy *kekosongan*
vacation *percutian*
vaccination *pemvaksinan*
vacuum cleaner *permbersih hampagas*
vagina *faraj*
vaginal infection *jangkitan faraj*
valid *sah laku*
valley *lurah*
valuable *bernilai*
value *nilai*
vegetable *sayur-sayuran*
vegetarian *tidak makan daging*
vehicle *kenderaan*
vehicle registration *pendaftaran kenderaan*
vending machine *mesin layan diri*
very *amat*
viewpoint [BE] *sudut pandangan*
village *kampung*
visa *visa*
visit v *melawat*
visiting hours *waktu melawat*
visually impaired *cacat penglihatan*
vitamin *vitamin*
V-neck *kolar V*
volleyball game *permainan bola tampar*
vomit v *muntah*

wait v *tunggu*
waist *pinggang*
waiter *pelayan lelaki*
waiting room *bilik menunggu*
waitress *pelayan perempuan*
wake v *bangun*
wake-up call *panggilan pagi*
walk v *berjalan*
wall clock *jam dinding*
wallet *dompet*
war memorial *tugu peringatan*
warm v **(something)** *memanaskan;* ~ adj **(temperature)** *panas*
wash v *membasuh; mencuci*
washing *machine mesin basuh*
watch *jam tangan*
water skis *ski air*
waterfall *air terjun*
watermelon *tembikai*
wear v *memakai*
weather *cuaca*
weave v *menganyam*
week *minggu;* ~**end** *hujung minggu*
weekly *setiap minggu*
welcome v *selamat datang*
well-rested *rehat secukupnya*
west *barat*
what *apa*
wheelchair *kerusi roda;* ~ **ramp** *tanjakan kerusi roda*
when *bila*
where *di mana*
white *putih*
who *siapa*

widowed *janda*
wife *isteri*
window *tingkap*
windsurfer *peluncur air*
wine list *senarai wain*
wireless internet service *kemudahan internet tanpa wayar*
wireless phone *telefon tanpa wayar*
with *dengan*
withdraw v *mengeluarkan*
withdrawal (bank) *pengeluaran*
without *tanpa*
woman *wanita*
wool *bulu kambing biri-biri*
work (function) *berfungsi*
work v *bekerja;* n *perkerjaan*
wrap v *membalut*
wrestling *perlawanan gusti*
wrist *pergelangan tangan*
write v *menulis;* n *tulisan*

Y

year *tahun*
yellow *kuning*
yes *ya*
yesterday *semalam*
yoghurt *yogurt*
you *anda; kamu*
you're welcome *sama-sama*
young *muda*
your *anda; kamu*
youth hostel *asrama belia*

Z

zoo *zoo*
zucchini *zukini*

Malay – English

A

ada *to be; to have*
abang *brother (older)*
adaptor *adapter*
adik *younger brother/sister*
aduan *complaint*
agar-agar *jelly (food)*
agensi *agency*
agensi perlancong *travel agency*
ahli kimia *chemist/pharmacist*
AIDS *AIDS*
air *water*
air bergas *sparkling water*
air kencing *urine*
air kolong *cologne*
air lemon *lemonade*
air minuman *drinking water*
air panas *hot water*
air terjun
air soda *soda*
air terjun *waterfall*
ais *ice*
akan *shall; will*
akaun *account*
akaun semasa *checking/current account*
akaun simpanan *savings account*
aku *I; me*
alah *allergic*
alamat *address*
alamat e-mel *e-mail address*
alasan *excuse; reason*
alat hawa dingin *air conditioning*
alat pengering rambut *hair dryer*
amat *very*
ambulans *ambulance*

Amerika Syarikat *United States (U.S.)*
anak *child*
anak sungai *stream*
anda *you; your*
anggota penyelamat *lifeguard*
anggur *grape*
anjing *dog*
anjing pemandu *guide dog*
antarabangsa *international*
antibiotik *antibiotic*
anting-anting *earrings*
apa *what*
apa khabar *how are you*
apa-apa *anything*
api *fire*
aprikot *apricot*
arah *direction*
arak *alcohol*
arang *charcoal*
arked *arcade*
arnab *rabbit*
aromaterapi *aromatherapy*
arteri *artery*
artritis *arthritis*
asli *authentic*
aspirin *aspirin*
asrama *dormitory*
asrama *hostel*
asrama belia *youth hostel*
ATM *ATM*
audio *audio*
automatik *automatic*
awal *early*
awam *public*
awas *danger*

ayah *father*
ayam *chicken/poultry*

B

baca; membaca *read*
badminton *badminton*
bagaimana *how*
bagasi *baggage/luggage*
bagasi tangan *hand luggage*
bagus *good*
bahagian *portion*
bahagian atas *upper*
bahagian kanak-kanak *children's portion*
bahan cuci *detergent*
bahan membersih *cleaning supplies*
bahasa *language*
bahaya *dangerous*
bahu *shoulder*
baik *good; nice*
baik hati *kind (person)*
baju *dress; clothing*
baju hujan *raincoat*
baju kemeja-T *T-shirt*
baju panas *sweater*
baju renang *swimsuit*
baju tidur *pajamas*
bakon *bacon*
bakul *basket (for groceries)*
balai polis *police station*
balang *jar*
balet *ballet*
balikan *reverse*
bandar *town*
bangun *wake v*
bangunan *building*
bank *bank*
bantal *pillow*
bar *bar (place)*

bar snek *snack bar*
barang kemas *jewelry*
barangan *goods*
barangan rumah *household goods*
barat *west*
barbeku *barbecue*
barisan *line; queue*
baru *new*
baru belajar *novice (skill level)*
bas *bus*
basikal *bicycle*
basikal berenjin *moped*
batal *clear v*
bateri *battery*
batuk *cough*
bawah tanah *subway/underground*
bawang putih *garlic*
bayam *spinach*
bayaran *fee*
bayaran balik *refund*
bayaran masuk *admission/cover charge*
bayi *baby*
bebas *free*
bebas cukai *duty-free*
bebas lemak *fat free*
beg *bag*
beg galas *backpack*
beg pakaian *suitcase*
beg sampah *garbage bag*
beg tangan *carry-on; handbag*
beg tidur *sleeping bag*
bekerja *work*
belajar *learn*
belajar *study*
belakang *back (body part); behind (direction)*
belanga *clay pot*

belanja *treat (to a drink)*
belimbing *carambola [starfruit]*
benar *real*
bengkak *swelling*
berais *icy*
berani *brave*
berapa *how much (price)*
bercakap *speak*
bercerai *divorce*
berdarah *bleed*
berdekatan *nearby*
berenang *swim*
berfungsi *work (function)*
berhenti *stop*
berhubungan *contact*
beri *to give*
beri jalan *give way (on the road)*
berjalan *to walk*
berjangkit *contagious*
berkhemah *to camp*
berlepas *to depart (planes)*
berlian *diamond*
bermain *to play*
bermalam *overnight*
bermula *to begin*
bernafas *breathe*
bernilai *valuable*
berpandangan dekat *near-sighted*
berpisah *separated (marriage)*
berplumbum *leaded (fuel)*
bersalut serbuk roti *breaded (cooking method)*
bersara *retired*
berseronok *fun*
bersolek *make up (face)*
bertaruh *bet*
bertemu *meet (someone)*

bertentangan *opposite*
berterima kasih *to thank*
bertolak *depart (bus/train)*
bertunang *engaged (in a relationship)*
berus rambut *hairbrush*
besar *big; large*
besbol *baseball*
betik *papaya (fruit)*
biara *monastery*
biasa *regular (normal)*
bibir *lip*
bijian *cereal*
bila *when*
bilik *room*
bilik air *bathroom*
bilik bujang *single room*
bilik kelamin *double room*
bilik mencuba pakaian *fitting room*
bilik menunggu *waiting room*
bilik mesyuarat *meeting room*
bir *beer*
biru *blue*
bising *loud*
blaus *blouse*
bola keranjang *basketball*
bola sepak *soccer*
boleh *to be able; can*
bomba *fire brigade*
borang *form (fill-in)*
bosan *boring*
bot keselamatan *life boat*
bot *boat*
botol *bottle*
brek *brakes (car)*
brokoli *broccoli*
buah-buahan *fruit*
buah dada *breast*

buah delima *pomegranate*
buah mangga *mango*
buah nangka *jackfruit*
buah pinggang *kidney (body part)*
buah zaitun *olive*
bubur *porridge*
budak *child*
budak lelaki *boy*
bujang *single (unmarried)*
buka *open*
bukan *not*
bukit *hill*
buku *book*
buku panduan *guide book*
bulan *month*
bulu kambing biri-biri *wool*
bunga *flower*
bungkus *take away (food)*
bungkusan *package*
burung *bird*
busuk *rotten*
butiran *itemize*

C

cacat *handicap*
cacat pendengaran *hearing impaired*
cadangan *recommendation*
cantik *beautiful*
cawan *cup*
cawan ukuran *measuring cup*
cecair *liquid*
cecair pencuci kanta sentuh
  contact lens solution
cecair pencuci pinggan mangkuk
  dishwashing liquid
cecincin kunci *key ring*
cek *check/cheque*
cek kembara *traveler's check*

cendawan *mushroom*
cenderahati *souvenir*
cenuram *cliff*
cepat *fast*
cerah *sunny*
ceri *cherry*
cermin mata *glasses/spectacles*
cermin mata hitam *sunglasses*
cerut *cigar*
cetakan gambar digital *digital print*
Cik *Miss*
cincin *ring*
cinta *love*
cirit-birit *diarrhea*
coklat *chocolates*
coli *bra*
comel *cute*
cuaca *weather*
cucu *grandchild*
cucu-cicit *grandchildren*
cukai *duty (tax)*
cukai jualan *sales tax*
cukai penerbangan *airport tax*
curam *steep*

D

dada *chest (body part)*
daging awet *cured meat*
daging babi *pork*
daging lembu *beef*
dahaga *thirsty*
dalam *in; inside*
dalam rumah *indoor*
dapur *kitchen; stove*
darah *blood*
darjah *degrees (temperature)*
datang *come*
datuk *grandfather*

daun *leaf*
daun bawang *scallion [spring onion]*
daun kari *curry leaves*
dekat *near*
delikatesen *delicatessen*
deman *fever*
deman alergi *hay fever*
denai *trail*
denda *fine (fee)*
dengan *with*
dewan *hall*
dewan bandar *town hall*
dewan persidangan *convention hall*
di luar *outside*
di mana *where*
di sebalik *around (the corner)*
di selekoh *on the corner*
dia *he, it, she*
dijual di kaunter *over the counter (medication)*
dikukus *steamed (cooking method)*
dilarang merokok *no smoking*
dingin *cool (temperature)*
dirompak *robbed*
diskaun *discount*
ditiup kering *blow-dry (hair)*
doktor *doctor*
doktor gigi *dentist*
doktor pakar kanak-kanak *pediatrician*
doktor pakar puan *gynecologist*
dolar *dollar*
domestik *domestic*
dompet *wallet*
dompet wanita *purse*
duduk *sit*
duit syiling *coin*
duit *money*

E

ekor *tail*
ekspres *express*
emak *mother*
emas *gold*
e-mel *e-mail*
Encik *Mr/Sir*
epal *apple*
epilepsi *epilepsy*
esok *tomorrow*

F

faham *understand*
faraj *vagina*
farmasi *pharmacy*
feri *ferry*
filem *film (camera)*
fonkepala *headphones*
fotografi *photography*
fotokopi *photocopy*

G

gabus *cork*
gadis *girl*
gambar *photo*
ganggu *bother; harass*
garaj *garage*
garis *line*
garpu *fork*
gas memasak *cooking gas*
gaung *ravine*
gaya *style (hair)*
gelanggang *court (sports)*
gelap *dark*
gelas *glass (drinking)*
gembira *happy*
gerai surat khabar *newsstand*
gereja *church*
gerobok *locker*

gigi *tooth*
gigi palsu *denture*
gigitan *bites*
gigitan serangga *insect bite*
gim *gym*
goreng *fried (cooking method)*
gua *cave*
gula *sugar*
gula-gula *candy*
gula-gula getah *chewing gum*
gunting *scissors*
gunung *mountain*

H

haba *heat*
hadiah *gift*
hai *hi*
haid *menstruation*
haiwan *animal*
hak lalu-lalang *right of way*
halal *permissible according to Islamic law*
hamil *pregnant*
hanya *only*
harga *cost; price*
hari *day*
hari ini *today*
hari jadi *birthday*
hasil tenusu *dairy*
hati *liver (body part)*
helo *hello*
hiburan *entertainment*
hidangan *meal*
hidangan sampingan *side dish*
hidangan utama *main course*
hidung *nose*
hijau *green*
hilang *lose (something)*
hilang dan terjumpa *lost and found*

hirisan *slice (of something)*
hitam *black*
hodoh *ugly*
hoki *hockey*
hoki ais *ice hockey*
hubungan *relationship*
hujan *rain*
hujung minggu *weekend*
hutan *forest*
hutan hujan *rainforest*

I

ialah *is*
ibu *mother*
ikan *fish*
ikan todak *swordfish*
imigrasi *immigration*
Inggeris *English*
ini *this*
insurans *insurance*
internet wayarles *wireless internet*
invois *invoice*
istana *palace*
istana kota *castle*
isteri *wife*
istimewa *special*
itik *duck (animal)*
itu *that*

J

jabatan api dan bomba *fire department*
jadual pertukaran *conversion table*
jadual waktu *schedule; timetable*
jagung *corn (vegetable)*
jaket *jacket*
jaket keselamatan *life jacket*
jalan *road*
jalan basikal *bike route*
jalan sehala *one-way street*

jalan yang lain *alternate route*
jam *clock; hour*
jam dinding *wall clock*
jam loceng *alarm clock*
jam tangan *watch*
jambatan *bridge*
janda *widowed*
jangan *do not*
jangka masa *period (of time)*
jangkitan *infection*
janji temu *appointment*
jauh *far*
jauh ke dalam *deeply*
jed *jade*
jem *jam (food)*
juga *too*
jumlah *total (amount)*
jururawat *nurse*
jurusan *stream (school)*
juruwang *cashier*
jus *juice*
jantan *male*
jantung *heart*
jarang *rare (object)*
jari *finger*
jari kaki *toe*

K

kabin *cabin*
kaca *glass (material)*
kacang *nuts (food)*
kacang pis *pea*
kacang soya *soy bean*
kad *card*
kad keahlian *membership card*
kad kredit *credit card*
kad kunci *key card*
kad memori *memory card*

kad pengenalan *identification card*
kad perniagaan *business card*
kad tambah nilai *top up card*
  (phone value)
kad telefon *phone card*
kadar *rate (exchange rate)*
kafe *café*
kain *fabric*
kain cadar *sheet*
kain kotor *laundry*
kain lampin *diaper*
kakak *elder sister*
kaki *foot; leg*
kalori *calories*
kambing *lamb (meat)*
kamera *camera*
kampung *village*
kamu *you; your*
kanak-kanak *child*
kanan *right (direction)*
kandang *main playpen*
kanta *lens*
kanta sentuh *contact lens*
kapal terbang *airplane*
kapas *cotton*
karton *carton*
kasino *casino*
kastam *customs*
kastam dan imigresen *passport control*
kasut *shoes*
kasut bertumit tinggi *high-heels*
kasut but *boots*
kasut lepak *loafers*
kasut sukan *sneaker*
kata laluan *password*
katil *bed*
katil bayi *crib*

katil bujang *single bed*
katil kelamin *double bed*
Katolik *Catholic*
kaunter *counter*
kawan *friend*
kawasan berkelah *picnic area*
kawasan hutan simpan *nature preserve*
kawasan membeli-belah *shopping area*
kawasan merokok *smoking area*
ke dalam *into*
keadaan *condition (medical)*
kecemasan *emergency*
kecil *small*
kecil *molek petite*
kecurian *theft*
kedai *store*
kedai cenderahati *souvenir store*
kedai dobi layan diri *laundromat*
kedai mainan *toy store*
kedai mencuci kering *dry cleaner*
kedai roti *bakery*
store kedai runcit *grocery*
kedai serbaneka *department store*
kegunaan *luar external use*
kejang datang haid *cramps (menstruation)*
keju *cheese*
kekosongan *vacancy*
kelab *club*
kelab malam *nightclub*
kelab menari *dance club*
kelab muzik jaz *jazz club*
kelabu *gray*
kelas *class*
kelas ekonomi *economy class*
kelas perniagaan *business class*
kelas pertama *first class*

kelengkapan *equipment*
kelengkapan menyelam *diving equipment*
kelengkapan snorkel *snorkeling equipment*
keluar *exit*
keluarga *family*
kemalangan *accident*
kemeja *shirt*
kemudahan *facility*
kenderaan *vehicle*
kentang *potato*
kepah *clam*
kepala *head (body part)*
kepeningan *drowsiness*
keping *piece*
keputusan *decision*
kerajang aluminium *aluminum foil*
keramat *Malay shrine*
kerang-kerangan *shellfish*
kereta *car*
kereta api bawah tanah *subway*
kereta sewa *rental car*
kereta sorong bayi *stroller*
keretapi *train*
kerongkong *throat*
kerongsang *brooch*
kertas *paper*
kertas tisu *paper towel*
kerusi *chair*
kerusi budak *child's seat*
kerusi roda *wheelchair*
kerusi tinggi budak *highchair*
kesan sampingan *side effect*
keselamatan *security*
kesesakan *congestion*
kesihatan *health*

kesilapan *mistake*
kesuntukan masa *rush (in a rush)*
ketam *crab (animal)*
ketat *tight*
keterangan *information*
ketibaan *arrivals (airport)*
ketinggian *height*
ketuhar gelombang mikro *microwave*
kewarganegaraan *nationality*
khabar baik *fine (greetings)*
khemah *camping; tent*
kipas *fan (appliance)*
kiri *left (direction)*
kitar semula *recycling*
kod kawasan *area code*
kod negara *country code*
kod pakaian *dress code*
kola *cola*
kolam *pond*
kolam renang *swimming pool*
kolam renang luar *outdoor pool*
kolan renang dalaman *indoor pool*
kolar *collar*
komputer *computer*
kondom *condom*
konsert *concert*
kopi *coffee*
kosong *empty*
kot *coat*
kota *fort*
kotak *box*
kotor *dirty*
krim *cream; ointment*
krim cukur *shaving cream*
krystal *crystal*
kuali *wok*
kuali leper *frying pan*

kualiti *quality*
kubis *cabbage*
kubis bunga *cauliflower*
kuil *temple (religious)*
kuku *nail*
kuku jari *fingernail*
kuku kaki *toenail*
kulit *leather; skin*
kumpulan *group*
kunci *key*
kunci bilik *room key*
kuning *yellow*
kuning air *beige*
kuprum *copper*
kurang *less*
kurang upaya *handicapped*
kurma *date (fruit)*

L

laci *drawer*
lada *pepper*
lada benggala *capsicum*
ladang *farm*
lalat *fly (insect)*
laluan pejalan kaki *walking route*
lampu *lamp*
lampu isyarat *traffic light*
lampu suluh *flashlight*
landasan *track (train)*
lantai *floor*
lapanpan terbang *airport*
lapar *hungry*
laporan polis *police report*
lari; melari *run*
lauk-pauk *dishes (food)*
laut *sea*
lawatan *sightseeing tour*
layan diri *self-service*

lebih *more*
lebih baik *better*
lebih besar *bigger*
lebih cepat *faster*
lebih kecil *smaller*
lebih murah *cheaper*
lebih perlahan *slower*
lebihan *excess*
lebuhraya *highway*
leher *neck*
lelaki *man*
lembu *ox*
lengan panjang *long sleeves*
lengan pendek *short sleeves*
lesen *licence*
letih; keletihan *tired; exhausted*
lewat *late (time)*
liat *tough (food)*
lidah *tongue*
lif *lift*
limau bali *pomelo*
limau gedang *grapefruit*
limau nipis *lime*
liter *liter*
lobak merah *carrot*
lobak putih *radish*
lokar *locker*
lorong *alley; path*
losen *lotion*
losen pelingdung matahari *sunblock*
losen selepas bercukur *aftershave*
lucu *funny*
lukis; melukis *draw*
lukisan *painting*
lurah *valley*
lurus *straight*
lutut *knee*

M

maaf *sorry*
maafkan saya *excuse me*
mabuk *drunk*
mabuk gerakan *motion sickness*
mabuk kembara *travel sickness*
mahal *expensive*
mainan *toy*
majalah *magazine*
makan *eat*
makan malam *dinner*
makan tengah hari *lunch*
makanan *food*
makanan bayi *baby food*
makanan laut *seafood*
makanan segara *fast food*
makanan tin *canned good*
maklumat *information*
malam *night*
malam ini *tonight*
malam tadi *last night*
malas *lazy*
mancis *match*
mandi *shower*
mangga *lock*
mangkuk *bowl*
manis *sweet (taste)*
masa *time*
masak *sauteed (cooking method)*
masalah *problem*
masam *sour*
masin *salty*
masjid *mosque*
masuk *access; enter*
mata *eye*
mata air panas *hot spring*
mata wang *currency*

matahari *sun*
mee *noodles*
meja *table*
mekanik *mechanic*
mel udara *airmail*
melampau *overdone*
melancong *tour*
melarang *prohibit*
melawat *visit*
melawat tempat-tempat *sightseeing*
Melayu *Malay*
meletak *to park (car)*
melihat *see*
melihat *look*
memadam *delete*
memakai *wear*
memanas *heating*
memanaskan *warm*
memandu *drive*
memandu melebihi had laju *speeding*
memanggang *roast*
memasak *cook*
memasukkan *deposit; insert*
membaiki *fix; mend*
membakar *bake; burn*
membalut *wrap*
membasuh *wash*
membatalkan *cancel*
membawa *bring*
membayar *to be charged; to pay*
membeli *buy*
membeli-belah *shop; shopping*
membenarkan *allow; permit*
memberhentikan sambungan
    disconnect (computer)
memberi *give*
membersihkan *clean*

memeluk *hug*
memepat *trim*
memeriksa *check*
memerlukan *need*
memesan *order*
meminda *alter*
mempamerkan *display*
memperbaiki *repair*
memperkenalkan *introduce*
mempreskripsikan *prescribe*
menaiki *board*
menaip *type*
menakjubkan *magnificent*
menambah *fill up (food)*
menangguh *delay*
menara *tower*
menari *dance*
menarik *attractive; interesting; pull*
mencabut *extract (tooth)*
mencadangkan *recommend*
mencetak *print*
mencium *kiss*
mencuri *steal*
mendaftar keluar *check-out*
mendaftar masuk *check-in*
mendail *dial*
mendapatkan *have*
menelan *swallow*
menelefon *phone*
menempah *book; reserve*
menerima *accept; receive*
mengadu *complain*
mengagumkan *amazing*
mengahwini *marry*
mengambil *take (something)*
mengandungi *contain*
menganyam *weave*

mengayuh basikal *cycling*
mengecap *stamp (postage)*
mengecas semula *recharge*
mengeja *spell*
mengeluarkan *withdraw*
mengemas *pack*
mengembalikan *return (something)*
mengembara tumpang *hitchhike*
mengesahkan *confirm*
menggunakan *use*
menggunting *cut (hair)*
menghadiri *attend*
menghantar *send*
menghantar dengan kapal *ship (mail)*
menghantar faks *fax*
menghantar surat *mail*
menghantar teks *text (send a message)*
menghubungi *notify*
menginap *stay*
mengisi *fill out (form)*
mengisytiharkan *declare*
mengukir *engrave*
mengukur *measure*
mengulangi *repeat*
mengunci *lock up*
mengutip *pick up (something)*
menikmati *enjoy*
menjadi *be*
menjual *sell*
menolak *to decline (credit card); to push*
mentah *raw*
mentega *butter*
menterjemah *translate*
mentol *lightbulb*
menu dengan harga tetap *fixed-price menu*
menu kanak-kanak *children's menu*
menu minuman *drink menu*
menukar *exchange; transfer (trains/flights)*
menukar *change*
menulis *write*
menunjukkan *show*
menyambung *connect (internet)*
menyebut *pronounce*
menyelam *dive*
menyertai *join*
menyeterika *to iron (clothes)*
menyewa *hire; rent*
menyewa kereta *car hire*
menyuap *feed*
merah *red*
merah jambu *pink*
meriah *gay (happy)*
merokok *smoke*
merompak *to mug; to rob*
merosakkan *damage*
message mesej segera *instant*
mesin basuh *washing machine*
mesin basuh pinggan mangkuk *dishwasher*
mesin layan diri *vending machine*
mesra kurang upaya *handicapped-accessible*
mesyuarat *meeting*
minat *interested*
minggu *week*
minggu yang lalu *last week*
minit *minute*
minta maaf *sorry*
minum *drink*
minuman *beverage*
minyak *gas; oil*

minyak diesel *diesel*
minyak tanpa plumbum *unleaded (gas)*
minyak wangi *perfume*
Misa *mass (church service)*
monorel *monorail*
motorbot *motor boat*
motorsikal *motorcycle*
muat *fit (clothing)*
muda *young*
muka *face*
muka surat *pages (in a book)*
mulut *mouth*
muntah *vomit*
murah *cheap*
mutiara *pearl*
muzik *music*
muzik klasik *classical music*
muzik rakyat *folk music*
muzium *museum*

N

nama *name*
nanas *pineapple*
nanti *later*
napkin *napkin*
nasi *rice*
negara *country*
nenek *grandmother*
nilai *value*
nombor *number*
nombor faks *fax number*
nombor lesen memandu *driver's license number*
nombor pengenalan diri *personal identification number (PIN)*
nombor telefon *phone number*
nota *notes*

O

orang *person*
orang Amerika *American*
orang British *British*
orang Cina *Chinese (person)*
orang Ireland *Irish*
orang tua *senior citizen*
orang yang baru belajar *beginner (skill level)*
oren *orange (color)*
orkestra *orchestra*
otot *muscle*

P

padamkan *turn off (lights)*
padang *field (sports)*
padang golf *golf course*
pagi *a.m./morning*
paha *thigh*
pakai buang *disposable*
pakaian dalam *underwear*
pakaian *clothing*
pakar *expert/specialist*
pakar optik *optician*
pakar runding *consultant*
panas *hot (temperature)*
pancuran air *fountain*
panggil *call*
panggilan pagi *wake-up call*
panggilan pindah bayaran *collect call*
panggung wayang *movie theater*
pangsapuri *apartment*
panjang *long*
pantai *beach*
papan luncur air *surfboard*
papan panduan kedai *store directory*
paru-paru *lung*
pas masuk *boarding pass*

pasangkan *turn on (lights)*
pasar *market*
pasar malam *night market*
pasar raya *mall; supermarket*
pasport *passport*
pasukan *team*
patah *broken (bone)*
patung *doll*
payung *umbrella*
pecah *break*
pedas *spicy*
pegang *hold*
peguam *lawyer*
pejabat *office*
pejabat konsul *consulate*
pejabat maklumat pelancong *tourist information office*
pejabat pos *post office*
pejalan kaki *pedestrian*
pekak *deaf*
pelajar *student*
pelancong *tourist*
pelantar *platform*
pelayan lelaki *waiter*
pelayan perempuan *waitress*
pelik *strange*
pelocok *plunger*
peluncur air *windsurfer*
pemanas *heater*
pemandu *guide (tourist)*
pemanis tiruan *artificial sweetener*
pemarut *grater*
pembalut *bandage*
pembalut plastik *plastic wrap*
permbersih hampagas *vacuum cleaner*
pembuka botol *bottle opener*
pembuka selera *appetizer; starter*

pembuka tin *can opener*
pemetik api *lighter*
pemvaksinan *vaccination*
pencukur pakai buang *disposable razor*
pencuri *thief*
pendaftaran kenderaan *vehicle registration*
pendandan rambut *hairstylist*
pendek *short*
penerbangan *flight*
penerbangan antarabangsa *international flight*
penerbangan domestik *domestic flight*
pengajaran *lesson (learnt a lesson)*
penganggur *unemployed*
pengasuh bayi *babysitter*
pengeluaran *withdrawal (bank)*
pengetahuan *knowledge*
penghalau serangga *insect repellent*
pengimbas *scanner*
penginapan *accommodation*
pengukus *steamer*
pengurus *manager*
pengurutan *massage*
pengurutan sukan *sports massage*
pening *dizzy*
penisilin *penicillin*
penjual bunga *florist*
penjual daging *butcher*
penterjemahan *interpreter*
penting *urgent*
penuh *full*
penumpang *passenger*
penyahbau *deodorant*
penyakit anemia *anemic*
penyakit kelamin *sexually transmitted disease*

penyakit kencing manis *diabetes*
penyakit lelah *asthma*
penyaman udara *air conditioning*
penyapu *broom*
penyejuk beku *freezer*
penyeliaan *supervision*
penyembur rambut *hairspray*
penyepit *chopsticks*
penyerlah *highlights (hair)*
pepijat *bug*
perang *brown*
perak *silver*
perak tulen *sterling silver*
perapi *conditioner (hair)*
perbatuan *mileage*
percutian *holiday*
percutian *vacation*
perempuan *female; woman*
pergelangan tangan *wrist*
pergerakan *mobility*
pergi *go (somewhere)*
perhentian bas *bus stop*
periuk *pot*
perjalanan *trip*
perkakas *utensil*
perkhidmatan *service (in a restaurant)*
perkhidmatan penuh *full-service*
perlahan-lahan *slowly*
perlawanan bola sepak *football game*
perlawanan gusti *wrestling*
perlepasan *departure*
permainan *game*
permainan bola tampar *volleyball game*
perniagaan *business*
perpustakaan *library*
persiaran dengan bas *bus tour*

persidangan *conference*
persimpangan *intersection*
pertama *first*
pertandingan golf *golf tournament*
pertandingan tinju *boxing match*
pertolongan *help*
pertukaran wang asing *currency exchange*
perut *stomach*
pesanan *message*
peta *map*
peta bandar *town map*
peta jalan *road map*
petang *evening; p.m.*
peti *box*
pintu keluar kecemasan *emergency exit*
pintu masuk *entrance*
pintu penghadang api *fire door*
pir *pear*
pisang *banana*
pisau *knife*
piuter *pewter*
poket *pocket*
pokok *tree*
polis *police*
porselin *porcelain*
pos *post*
poskad *postcard*
potongan rambut *haircut*
preskripsi *prescription*
Puan *Madam/Mrs*
puing *ruins*
pukul *o'clock*
puncak *peak (of a mountain)*
pundi kencing *bladder*
punggung *buttocks*
pusat *center*

putih *white*
puting *pacifier*

R

rabun *blur; dim*
rabun dekat *long-sighted*
rabun jauh *short-sighted*
racun *poison*
rahang *jaw*
rakan *colleague; friend*
ramalan *forecast*
rambut *hair*
rancangan *plan*
rantai *chain*
rantau *region*
rasa *taste*
rasa mual *nauseous*
ratu *queen*
rawatan kaki *pedicure*
rawatan muka *facial*
reaksi alah *allergic reaction*
rebus *boil (cooking method)*
rehat *rest*
rendah *low*
reneh *poach (cooking method)*
resit *receipt*
restoran *restaurant*
ribut petir *thunderstorm*
rogol *rape*
rokok *cigarette*
romantis *romantic*
rombongan *excursion*
rosak *break down*
roti *bread*
ruam *rash*
ruang makan *dining room*
rumah *home; house*
rumpai laut *seaweed*

S

sabun *soap*
saderi *celery*
sah laku *valid*
sains *science*
saiz *size*
saiz tambah *plus size*
sakit *hurt; ill; pain; unwell*
sakit dada *chest pain*
sakit jantung *heart condition*
sakit kepala *headache*
sakit kerongkong *sore throat*
sakit perut *stomachache*
sakit perut akibat haid *menstrual cramp*
sakit telinga *earache*
salji *snow*
salun *salon*
saluran elektrik *electric outlet*
sama *the same; identical*
sama-sama *you're welcome*
sambilan *part-time*
sambungan *connection; extension*
sampah *rubbish; trash*
sampul surat *envelope*
sana *there*
sandiwara *play (theatre)*
sangat *really*
sarapan pagi *breakfast*
sari kata *subtitle*
sarung kaki *sock*
sarung kamera *camera case*
satu *one*
saya *I; me*
sayur-sayuran *vegetable*
se- *per*
sebelah *next to*
sebelum *before*

sedang menari *dancing*
sedang menjalin hubungan *attached (in a relationship)*
sedap *delicious*
sederhana *medium (size)*
sedia *ready*
sedih *sad*
sedikit *little; some*
segar *fresh*
sehala *one-way (ticket)*
sehar *per day*
sejam *per hour*
sejuk *cold; cool*
sekali *once*
sekarang *now*
sekolah *school*
selada *lettuce*
selamat datang *welcome*
selamat jalan *goodbye*
selamat pagi *good morning*
selamat petang *good evening*
selamat tengah hari *good afternoon*
selaran matahari *sunburn*
selatan *south*
selekoh *corner*
selepas *after*
selimut *blanket*
selipar *slippers*
selsema *cold (sickness)*
seluar dalam *briefs (clothing)*
seluar panjang *pants*
seluar pendek *shorts*
semalam *yesterday*
semasa *during*
sembelit *constipated*
sementara *temporary*
seminggu *per week*

semula *again*
senang *easy*
senarai *list*
sendi *joint (body part)*
sendirian *alone*
sengat *sting*
serai *lemongrass*
serangan *attack (on person)*
servis bilik *room service*
sesat *lost*
sesiapa *anyone*
setengah *half*
seterusnya *next*
setiap minggu *weekly*
sewa kereta *car rental*
siapa *who*
sibuk *busy*
sijil *certificate*
sikat *comb*
siku *elbow*
sila *please*
simpan *keep; save*
simpan sejuk *keep refrigerated*
sini *here*
sirap *syrup*
sisa-sisa *traces*
sistem penerbangan *airline*
snek *snacks*
soalan *question*
sos *sauce*
sosej *sausage*
sotong *squid*
sotong kurita *octopus*
spesimen *specimen*
stesen *station*
stensen bawah tanah *underground station*

stesen keretapi *train station*
stesen minyak *gas station*
stik *steak*
strawberi *strawberry*
strok matahari *sunstroke*
suami *husband*
sudu *spoon*
sudu teh *teaspoon*
sudu ukuran *measuring spoon*
sudut pandangan *viewpoint*
suhu *temperature*
suka *like*
sukan *sports*
sungai *river*
sungguh *really*
sunyi *quiet*
sup *soup*
surat *letter*
surat berdaftar *registered mail*
surat khabar *newspaper*
susah *difficult*
susu *milk*
sut *suit*
sutera *silk*
syampu *shampoo*
syarikat *company; firm*

T

tahu *know*
tahun *year*
tajam *sharp*
tali leher *tie (clothing)*
tali pinggang *belt*
tali sawat penyampai *conveyor belt*
taman *garden*
taman hiburan *amusement park*
taman permainan *playground*

tamat *end*
tambahan *extra*
tambang *fare (charge)*
tampalan *filling (tooth)*
tandas *restroom; toilet*
tandatangan *signature*
tangan *arm; hand*
tangga *stairs*
tangga gerak *elevator*
tanggal *take off (clothes)*
tanjakan *ramp*
tanpa *without*
tanpa diawasi *unattended*
tanpa had *unlimited*
tanpa wayar *wireless*
tapak perkhemahan *campsite*
tarik nafas *breathe deeply*
tarikh *date (calendar)*
tarikh lupus *expiration date*
tasik *lake*
tauhu *bean curd*
tawar *bland*
tayar *tire/tyre*
teh *tea*
tekanan darah *blood pressure*
teksi *taxi*
telah berkahwin *married*
telah dicuri *stolen*
telah rosak *damaged*
telefon *telephone*
telefon awam *pay phone*
telefon mudah alih *cell phone*
televisyen *TV*
telinga *ear*
telur *egg*
teman lelaki *boyfriend*
teman wanita *girlfriend*

tembikai *watermelon*
tembikar *pottery (goods)*
tempahan *reservation*
tempat *place*
tempat berlabuh *berth*
tempat duduk *seat*
tempat duduk tepi lorong *aisle seat*
tempat meletak kereta *parking lot*
tempat menarik *attraction (place)*
tempat peranginan *resort (holiday)*
tempat pertempuran *battleground*
tempat tarikan utama *main attraction*
tempatan *local*
tendang *kick*
tengah hari *afternoon; midday*
tengah malam *midnight*
tenis *tennis*
tepat masa *on-time*
terakhir *last*
terang *light (bright)*
terbaik *best*
terbang; menerbang *fly*
terima kasih *thank you*
terjangkit *infected*
termasuk *include*
terseliuh *sprain*
tertutup *closed*
teruk *terrible*
terung ungu *eggplant/aubergine*
terus *straight*
tiada *not have*
tiada apa-apa *nothing*
tiang *pole; post*
tiba *arrive; reach*
tidak makan daging *vegetarian*
tidak sedarkan diri *unconscious*

tidak *no*
tidur *sleep*
tikar *mat; rug*
tiket *ticket*
tiket elektronik *e-ticket*
tikus *rat*
timur *east*
tinggal *live*
tinggi *high*
tingkap *window*
tingkat *storey*
tisu tandas *toilet paper*
titik *drop (medicine)*
topi *hat*
topi keledar *helmet*
tradisional *traditional*
trak penarik *tow truck*
trek kuda *horse track*
troli *cart; trolley*
tua *old (person)*
tuala *towel*
tuala wanita *sanitary napkin*
tugu *statue*
tugu peringatan *war memorial*
tujuan *purpose*
tukang gunting rambut *barber*
tukul *hammer*
tulang *bone*
tulang belakang *spine (body part)*
tulang rusuk *rib (body part)*
tunggu *wait*
tuntutan bagasi *baggage claim*
turun *get off (a train/bus/subway)*
tutup *close (not open)*
tingkat bawah *ground floor*
tiram *oyster*
tisu *tissue*

U

ubat *medicine*
ubat bius *anesthesia*
ubat gigi *toothpaste*
ubat tahan *sakit painkiller*
udang *shrimp*
udang galah *lobster*
udara *air*
ukiran *carvings*
ulang-alik *round-trip*
umbai usus *appendix (body part)*
umur *age*
ungu *purple*
universiti *university*
untuk *for*
utara *north*

W

waktu *time*
waktu melawat *visiting hours*

wang *money*
wang kertas *currency note*
wang pendahuluan *cash advance*
wang tunai *cash*
wanita *lady; woman*
wap air *steam*
warga Australia *Australian*
warga Kanada *Canadian*
warna *color*
wayang *movie*

Y

ya *yes*
yang *the one which/whom*
yogurt *yoghurt*

Z

zaitun *olive*
zakar *penis*
zukini *zucchini*

Berlitz®

speaking your language

phrase book & dictionary
phrase book & CD

Available in: Arabic, Brazilian Portuguese*, Burmese*, Cantonese
Chinese, Croatian, Czech*, Danish*, Dutch, English, Filipino, Finnish*, French,
German, Greek, Hebrew*, Hindi*, Hungarian*, Indonesian, Italian, Japanese,
Korean, Latin American Spanish, Malay, Mandarin Chinese, Mexican Spanish,
Norwegian, Polish, Portuguese, Romanian*, Russian, Spanish, Swedish, Thai,
Turkish, Vietnamese
*Book only